WALKING ON THE
AND SOUTH DC

Walking on the North and South Downs

Mark Chapman

ROBERT HALE · LONDON

© Mark Chapman 1985
First published in Great Britain 1985

ISBN 0 7090 1866 5

Robert Hale Limited
Clerkenwell House
Clerkenwell Green
London EC1R OHT

TO MY PARENTS

Photoset in North Wales by
Derek Doyle & Associates, Mold, Clwyd
Printed in Great Britain by
St Edmundsbury Press, Bury St Emunds, Suffolk

Contents

KEY TO INDIVIDUAL WALK MAPS

Route of one direction walk

Route of circular walk

Towns, villages, hamlets

Farms, isolated buildings, etc

Main built-up areas

Woodland

Illustrations

All photographs taken by the author

1

Introduction

Most walking books tend to treat the North Downs in isolation from the South Downs – and the Greensand hills in between are rarely discussed. This is a pity, because the Downs of North and South are part of the same geological landform and are not isolated features. By acknowledging the link, it is possible to create a very long walk, almost entirely on hills, that enables an extensive exploration of the countryside of the South East.

The core of this book is a long-distance walk through the South East of England. The course of the walk describes, with a little imagination, the shape of a massive horseshoe. Beginning in Dover, it follows the North Downs across Kent and Surrey to Farnham, crosses the western Weald of Surrey and Sussex and then goes along the South Downs to Beachy Head. It begins and ends on the coast.

There might be a few people willing and able to undertake the walk in one continuous venture – in which case approximately three weeks are needed. However, the majority may wish to tackle it in a series of day trips or weekends. Others may prefer to take those parts of the walk that appeal most or to alter the order in which things are done (walk Sussex before Kent for example). Some might wish to return to the starting-point of each day's walk. The structure of the book is designed to meet all these needs.

The area covered by the entire walk is divided into six

'blocks' of country – East Kent, Medway, West Kent and Surrey, the Western Greensand Country, South Downs west of the Arun, and South Downs east of the Arun. These broad divisions are based largely upon the variation in the countryside between these areas: not dramatic, but noticeable.

The entire long-distance walk is broken down into individual walks that can be accomplished in a day. Each of these begins and ends at a point with public transport and accommodation readily available or readily accessible from that point. This enables either a continuation of the walk the next day or a means of returning home and coming back to the previous finishing-place the next time. Each day's walk can also be treated in isolation and thus the sequence of the long-distance walk may be changed to suit the individual.

Running concurrent with the above division, the long-distance route is also split into units, each of which can be completed in one day, where the walker can return to the point from which the day's walk began. It has been possible to create round-trip walks along most of the long-distance route (rather like links on a chain), so that each round-trip takes you a little further along the overall route each time. Unfortunately not all of the route can be divided up in this way, and some of the ground can only be covered using the one-direction walks in the main sequence – but in all cases it is ensured that public transport can be used to return to the start.

Here and there some short stretches of the long-distance route did not lend themselves to such a treatment, and there are occasional gaps in the route where it was not possible to cover the ground and return to a base.

Accommodation, public transport and car-parking are mentioned at the beginning or end of each walk, but no specific details are given. Facts are readily available from other sources (train and bus timetables, tourist information guides, etc.) and may in any case change frequently. But every walk has been planned with access a foremost consideration.

It is intended that the way-finding text be used in conjunction with the relevant OS 1:50,000 map. It would be unwise to rely solely on the maps given in this book; if you do go off the path and lack a detailed map, you could be well and truly lost. The maps here given might be looked up the night before the walk, the better to plan the route and learn the ground, thus saving tedious first-time reading in the field. For many of the walks, background information precedes the detailed account, and this too may be read separately – perhaps the night before.

This book is a practical guide for walkers. It assumes competence with a map and compass and sufficient experience of walking to know how to equip oneself. This sort of information is so readily available from so many other sources that it seemed pointless to take up space best used for describing as many walks as possible.

Many books on walking tend to forget most of what is to be seen in the countryside and concentrate on the highlights – the churches, the tourist villages and the birthplaces of the famous. Interesting enough, but what of the ninety per cent of the walk when none of this is relevant? I have tried to go some way to filling this gap by explaining the countryside as a whole to be seen on the walks. The seemingly commonplace can be fascinating once it is understood. A field is not just a field, and there is more to woodland than many are aware. Space precluded discussion of individual villages and other detail in this book; I believe the sheer volume of other books about the South East dealing with such matters justifies the omission.

The countryside to be experienced on these walks is almost everywhere fine. It is essentially a landscape of mixed farming, woodland and downland in the best traditions of the South East. The hilltop paths give long views over the subtly varied landscapes. It is a densely settled area, lived in for centuries, farmed, tended and built upon. Yet the walks are almost wholly rural and hardly ever leave open countryside.

But for all this, it is close to large centres of population. The route passes near to London, the Medway towns and the heavily developed South Coast. There are also large individual towns and cities throughout the region. In other words the walks are accessible to a very large urban population, whilst the urbanization, with a very few exceptions, remains clear of the route and is to all intents 'out of sight, out of mind'.

For most of the time you will be in countryside many miles from the nearest town, but even when you do pass near large settlements, their presence is rarely felt.

Important points need to be made about the sort of paths recommended in this book.

First, take special care when walking in woodland, National Trust land and any sort of area under general public use — commons, for example. This is because in these areas there are far more paths than the map would lead one to expect. New rides, fire-breaks and tracks are frequently being cut in woodland, and there is often a confusing mass of 'unofficial' paths on heavily used land. The instructions in this book try to steer around these problems, but do take extra care in such areas and be prepared for problems in map-reading.

Secondly, be prepared for times when the paths are impossible to see on the ground. The instructions point this out wherever possible, but many of the paths can be unclear in the under-used areas. Also, the clarity of a path is influenced by local conditions. For example, a recently ploughed field might show no traces of the path crossing it — yet you know it to be there. Unless a path follows a field edge or is in woodland, there are often occasions when its line will be ploughed out or planted over. Be ready for these occasions, and map-reading, together with the written notes, will see you right.

Thirdly, waymarking. This is generally good in the area concerned, and where it is deficient, the paths often make up for the failing by being clear. However, there are cases where it is appalling and you will have to rely on this book. Generally, serious problems over path clarity and waymarking are few, and it is hoped that the book will correct any doubts as they arise.

Finally, there are occasions when you will be walking on paths that are not shown on the map. This can be misleading and worrying. The reason for this is that some of the paths are new rights of way, created to make a link between pre-existing paths, and are therefore not on the map yet. This is particularly so in Kent on parts of the North Downs Way. In cases like this the waymarking and stiles on the ground are sufficient reassurance that you are on a path. However, remember this if on any occasion the place to which the book has guided you seems not to be a right of way.

In the walks we make use of a wide range of paths in a variety of settings, from the path on the cloud-shadowed hilltops to the lane winding deep between quiet hedgerows. On the circular walks and those across the Greensand country, many different routes are used, but on the continuous 'horseshoe' extensive use is made of the long-distance chalkland paths known as the North Downs Way and South Downs Way. Both these paths are of great antiquity, and although they both follow a line of chalk hills, their characters are very different.

It is impossible to say just how old a path is. Certainly the South Downs Way was in use during the New Stone Age (the neolithic) for there are remains from this time along the route. But even before this time a range of hills would have offered the best cross-country way, so it could well have been in use during the mesolithic period ten thousand years ago.

By the Bronze Age there was an established network of highways, and of these the path along the crest of the South Downs was undoubtedly a major one, offering dry passage above the Wealden forest. A second trail ran along the foot of the Downs to the north, roughly parallel for at least some of the way. Some remaining parts of this path are used on the walks. There must have been a network of lesser local tracks branching off these main routes – but which ones they are today is largely guesswork. However, paths running from any ancient landmark are likely to be very old. An example on the South Downs is the path between Cissbury and the South Downs Way – here there is both a hilltop fort and flint mines. Again, the map has a lot to offer in this speculative game.

Whereas the South Downs Way is a true hilltop path, sticking faithfully to the crest of the scarp, its North Downs equivalent is more varied. It is sometimes on top of the scarp, sometimes at the foot of it or even, in places, part way up the slope. This means that, when walking it, there are often switches from top to bottom of the slope as local conditions have influenced the line taken over the centuries.

The North Downs Way is probably equally as ancient as the South Downs Way. Parts of it are termed also the Pilgrims' Way, but while the overall direction taken by the pilgrims between Winchester and Canterbury would have been along this route, the exact line is unproven. Even so, pilgrimage would have been a comparatively minor use compared to the centuries of commercial traffic and travellers.

In prehistory the whole line of the North Downs from the Straits of Dover to Farnham (and beyond to Salisbury Plain) would have been very important. However, in historic times, the area between the Stour Gap (Wye) and the Channel fell from use as the emphasis of travel changed. (This was because the link from Winchester and Canterbury remained significant and actually grew in importance as the cities did. The section beyond to Dover was no longer important.)

Of course the whole North Downs as a route declined in importance as new transport links developed – just as the South Downs did – and new centres of economic activity grew up. Some use remained and does to this day. Indeed parts of the Way are still functional as surfaced roads. But the North Downs Way is a mixture of roads and paths – some of them neglected, some well used.

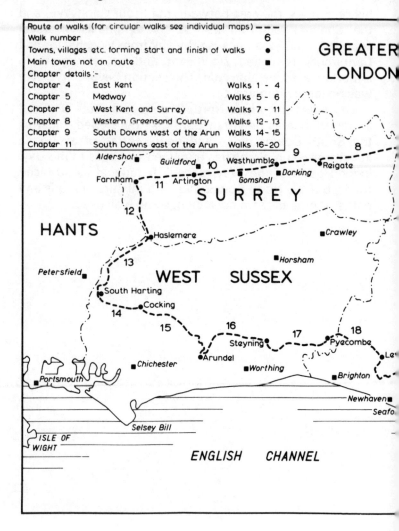

Route of walks (for circular walks see individual maps) — — —
Walk number   6
Towns, villages etc. forming start and finish of walks   ●
Main towns not on route   ■
Chapter details :-
Chapter 4   East Kent   Walks 1 - 4
Chapter 5   Medway   Walks 5 - 6
Chapter 6   West Kent and Surrey   Walks 7 - 11
Chapter 8   Western Greensand Country   Walks 12- 13
Chapter 9   South Downs west of the Arun   Walks 14- 15
Chapter 11   South Downs east of the Arun   Walks 16-20

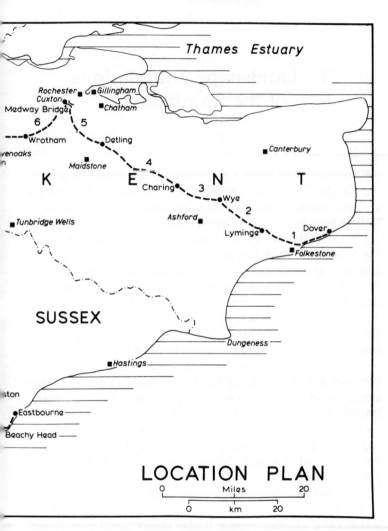

LOCATION PLAN

2

The Landscape Foundations
of the South East

It is important to have a general grasp of how the land in the South East was formed, for from this can stem an understanding of so much that is to be seen on the walk. Nature supplied the land which we have adapted to meet our needs, and however removed from its natural state the landscape may become, the way we use the land is still basically determined by its natural characteristics. The soil influences how we farm it, and the rock determines what we can quarry from it, just as the shape of the land decides where roads and towns can best be situated. Therefore it seems appropriate at this early stage to give a very general account of the basic form of the South East.

Fundamental to the explanation is that all the area between London and the English Channel is a part of the same enormous landform. In other words, the North Downs, South Downs and Weald, ending roughly at the Hampshire border, can all be seen together as a unit sharing a common geological heritage. This means that the course of the walk follows roughly the perimeter of this land area.

Initially the region was a large platform. This formed a base for sedimentary deposits collecting in the subsequent period. Firstly these layers were put down beneath a lake that covered the area, and later layers were put on top when the region was submerged under a sea. This deposition included sands, clays, chalk and ultimately more sands and clays. We are talking of an enormous timespan, a timescale so large that grains of sand, silt and sealife skeletons (chalk) could collect to depths of hundreds of feet and be compressed into rock.

After this period all of these layers were lifted up from beneath to make a massive dome. England was still joined to the Continent at this time, and the dome stretched all the way from France to Hampshire, and from where London now lies to the south coast area.

The uplifted dome was acted on by erosion. This would doubtless have been more rapid at the top than at the edges because of the weakened, fissured nature of the top resulting from the stresses of its uplift. The erosion 'hollowed out' the land within the edges of the dome.

The edges of the dome now remain as 'stumps' — the North and South Downs. The erosion of the dome has presently reached a point where the land between the North and South Downs is in general lower than these chalk hills. It is this area that can be termed 'The Weald' — the greater part of the land area of South East England.

It can be seen, looking at the present shape of the Downs, how they would once have been the lower slopes of a dome. Take, for example, the South Downs. There is a clearly defined steep slope on the northern side of the range of hills and a gentle slope dropping gradually away towards the sea on the southern side. It is easy to visualize this gentle slope (termed a dip slope) as part of the gradient down from the top of the dome somewhere over the central Weald. The steep slope (scarp slope) is created by the cutting back of the rock layers, by erosion, from the top of the dome outwards. This is still in progress.

The Weald contained within the rim of chalk is not a uniform area. This becomes apparent as the walk progresses. The Weald is comprised of layers that were once beneath the chalk covering and, like the chalk, were pushed up into a dome. Therefore they are layers tilted upwards and inwards towards the centre of the Weald.

Each rock band on the northern side of the Weald has its counterpart on the southern side, for they are the remaining stumps of the same curved layer.

Travel across the Weald in a north-south line and you cross 'bands' of sands or sandstones alternating with clays. Very generally, the sandstones are ridges, and the clays give rise to plains and vales.

One of these rocks is called Lower Greensand and is of major interest to us, for where it is constituted of hard bands it forms an especially resistant type of sandstone and as a result leads to hills and a distinctive scarp. As we walk along the North Downs, this scarp is apparent as a range of low hills stretching from near Maidstone westwards into Surrey as far as Redhill to the south of the Downs and roughly parallel to them.

Between Redhill and Dorking there is no marked hill range on the Greensand, and as a result we are conscious of long, uninterrupted views to the South Downs. West of Dorking the Greensand is again prominent as the Surrey Hills, and the highest hills in the South East are found here. Between Farnham and Haslemere we are walking on the massive ridge of Lower Greensand that curves along the Hampshire border between the North and South Downs.

When walking along the South Downs, although we are still walking parallel with the Lower Greensand running to the north of us, it is generally an indistinct feature. This is because the sandstone is softer there and has suffered more from erosion than its equivalent band in Kent and Surrey. Often when we are looking out across the Sussex Weald, the land appears only gently undulating. The only noticeable area of Greensand hills is in the vicinity of Petworth.

Between the foot of the Downs and the Greensand hills is an area largely of clay. For much of the length of the North Downs this forms a distinctive feature between the chalk hills to the north and those of the Greensand to the south because it appears as a valley between the two. Again, walking along the South Downs, it is unclear because of the lack of containing Greensand hills.

Moving inwards towards the centre of the Weald, then, we leave chalk and cross clay and then Greensand. Within the encircling Greensand is an extensive flat or gently undulating area of clay which more or less encloses the central sandstone heart of the Weald. This clay area is known as the Low Weald. The sandstone 'heartland' it encloses has resisted erosion and is the High Weald. The High Weald is generally more conspicuous as a rise in relief in the middle distance when viewed from the Sussex Downs. Viewed from the Surrey Downs and in western Kent, the Greensand ridge tends to obscure the longer view.

The most natural element in the South East landscape is the actual shape of the land itself — there is virtually nothing on the land surface that is unaltered by man. But, with minor exceptions such as quarries and road cuttings, the hills, plains, river gaps and sea cliffs are as nature made them.

So this, very generally, is the geological foundation of the counties of Sussex, Surrey and Kent; the bones of the landscape. Some of it may seem irrelevant, but its importance will gradually become obvious. There is much detail of interest to be introduced into the account as it is encountered on the walks. Hopefully, understanding the basics behind it all will make it clearer, more relevant and so more enjoyable.

3

Maps as Landscape Guides

When reading a map to find the way, you tend to build up an impression of the land through which the walk passes. Often this is of only a general nature – where the hills and woods are to be encountered, the rivers crossed and the villages met.

Yet an ordinary 1:50,000 OS map (let alone the larger scales available) such as will be used on these walks is a mass of information. It is possible to sit at home, miles from where the walks will take place, and build up a good picture of how the landscape will look when you do at last set foot in it. In addition to what is immediately obvious on the map – roads, woods, urban areas – informed guesses can be made of geology, the type of farmland, how the landscape may have developed through history and so on. (Specific examples will become apparent later in the book as the map is used in particular cases, e.g. the Ouse Gap). Maps are an invaluable tool in landscape interpretation.

Generally, then, how might this tool be used? Take an example – OS map 199, Eastbourne and Hastings. The only area of this map to be used on these walks is the south-west corner. However, reference may be made to the whole sheet on occasion.

The Shape of the land (its 'Morphology')
The morphology of an area is well shown by contour lines. But, even though the contour lines are the basis of

information on relief, the mass of other evidence should never be overlooked – these include spot heights, triangulation pillars and hachuring to show embankments.

But to return to contour lines. Look at the Downs between Alfriston and Bostal Hill (e.g. GR TQ497048). In this area two types of slope can be seen lying either side of the line created by the South Downs Way path. To the north-east of the path the contour lines are close together, so this is clearly a steep slope. However, south-west of the path the contour lines show a slope (dropping away south-westwards), but their wider spacing shows it to be a much gentler one than that to the north-west. So, in profile, this hill would look roughly like this:

Thus it can be seen that the map has enabled a picture of the shape of this land to be built up in the mind's eye. I am sure the sketch is what those familiar with the South Downs will recognize as the typical steep scarp and gentle dip slope profile of this range of hills.

Contour lines can be used to visualize the major landscape features of an area. For example, by following the line taken by the parallel contours, the scarp slope of the Downs is very clear where it runs between, say, Bostal Hill and Alfriston. Equally they are useful in showing up valleys (e.g. Grid Square TQ5002) as they trace the outline of the feature – this is particularly valuable in looking at dry valleys, where there is no stream to give them away.

The lack, or comparative lack, of contour lines is important evidence in itself. If there are none, as in the floor of the Cuckmere valley – then the land is flat or only rises and falls gently. If there are some widely spaced contours, as in the vicinity of the A27, then the land is only gently undulating. Both examples are typical Wealden relief.

Geology

Some geological types give so many map clues to their existence that there is almost an embarrassment of evidence. Others are less clear and can at best be narrowed down to a number of likely possibilities, although it might be possible to say what they definitely are not. Accurate geological maps are available if wanted, but even the 1:50,000 has a great deal to offer the landscape detective.

On the Eastbourne and Hastings map we know the Downs to be composed of chalk, but if this was not known, what might we tell by? Chalk is one of the easy ones. Look for dry valleys (Grid Square TQ5002) and coombes (GR TQ575026) where the contours show these; a general lack of surface water (streams, lakes, ponds, ditches); deliberately constructed dew ponds (GR TQ494046); streams beginning at the foot of the scarp — thus pointing to a spring-line where water has soaked into the chalk and emerged below it on meeting another rock (GR TQ499063). Place-name evidence is important too: look for names like 'down' (GR TQ535016), 'coombe' (GR TQ574021) or even the obvious 'chalk' in a farm name, for example. There might also be named chalk quarries or cement works.

The other main rock types of interest in the area covered by the walks are clay and sandstone, and these are less easy to tell.

Clay is commonly in a terrain of low relief — the contours will show this. It also holds water, so there is likely to be not only a stream network (and the streams will tend to have frequent meanders) but lakes, ponds, moated houses and so on. The fertility of the clay may have led to a dense pattern of rural settlement. This is all fairly general stuff, but put together it points towards a reasonably reliable conclusion. All of the above-mentioned features can be seen on the Eastbourne and Hastings sheet west of the A267 in the area south-west of Heathfield.

Sandstone is less easy to pinpoint, not least because it can occur in a variety of forms. There are many types of sandstone, and it can produce both low and high relief, poor and rich soils, dense and sparse settlement patterns. However, as a general rule in the South East, it coincides with land of comparatively high relief (indeed, it produces the highest land of the region), poor soil and hence under-use of the land by man. So again, look for contour-line evidence, lack of agricultural use (extensive woodlands and heaths) and, again place-name clues. These might include 'sand' or 'heath' and named sand workings. The Eastbourne and Hastings sheet displays some of these features in the vicinity of Heathfield.

There are other rock types to be met on the walk, but these are the main ones. Obviously prior knowledge is always a help. Knowing the South East to contain no rocks of some types will immediately eliminate them from speculation and thus aid the search for clues. In some cases it may even give a positive identification as there is only one possibility left.

Soils and 'natural' vegetation

Essentially, working out the soils and natural vegetation from a map is a matter of deduction from those assumptions already made about geology. There are a great many influences on the formation of soil – climate, relief, particular local conditions (such as periodic flooding) and, of course, the underlying rock from which the soil is normally derived. So if we can arrive at the rock type, we are well along the road to deducing soil type (we need not concern ourselves with climate over such a comparatively small and relatively unvaried climatic region of England).

There is little to beat knowledge of soils in this matter

(and gaining it by practical experience cannot be bettered) – you simply have to know what type of soil is found under what sort of geological condition. Use your eyes every time you are out, and the knowledge will come.

So geology is important. But the map can also offer other pointers. For example, suspect silt in flat valley floors such as that of the Cuckmere where river alluvium will have been laid down by floods. Or again, where there are heaths shown on the map, expect thin, poor and sandy soils. These are just random examples. Knowing what soil types to expect has a very practical value too, for it can point to likely conditions under foot. If you knew you were going to be walking on clay after rain, might you not change the plans?

Deducing the 'natural' vegetation is a matter of knowledge again. Observation of what sort of plant life exists in what sort of soil is the key here. There might be short cuts such as mention of a 'heath', indicating a particular variety of vegetation, but generally it is a case of a chain of reasoning: geology – soils – vegetation. Of course it might all be very misguided, because man will almost certainly have induced massive changes on the land, but here and there certain remnants of species occurring on particular soils should be found.

Present land uses
Much of this is obvious from simple familiarity with map symbols. From this will be learnt where woods, rivers, towns, roads and so on are situated. This is easy meat to any competent map-reader. But again, as so often, the map can yield up more secrets than those which are immediately obvious.

For example – woodland. There are a great many varieties of wood and forest in the countryside (and here I am thinking of the use to which the woodland is put, rather than just the species present). A dense network of tracks and rides in a wood (such as Friston Forest in the area east of the lower Cuckmere valley) clearly means that the area is open to access. This might be for recreation by the public and/or commercial forestry. Woods lacking such tracks, of which there are many on this map, are more likely to be unmanaged. The many long, straight edges to Friston Forest are also indicative of deliberate planting and management.

Farmland – this can be a very hazardous field of speculation. The best that can be hoped for is an idea of the predominant farmland type in a given area. You will need to know what conditions of relief, soil, climate and specific local factors (such as lack of water) favour particular farming practices – past experience in the field, again, here. Even then the map can give no clue on how a landowner chooses to use his land – market forces may well be far more significant than natural conditions in some cases. However, map evidence would suggest pasture in the drained lowlands beside the Cuckmere south of Alfriston. The inability to use machinery on steep slopes would suggest grassland rather than arable on the Downs scarp. These are comparatively easy. It becomes harder on the less determinate rolling land of the Downs or flat lands of the Weald. Having decided upon chalk geology on the Downs, and with past experience of chalkland, you should be able to guess at a predominance of arable land in large, open fields. Without this knowledge of the modern farming practices in chalk areas, you would, I fear, be in the dark – you might even expect to find the vast sheep pastures of the past.

So it does come down to the point that, in finding out the less obvious modern land uses from a map, a little knowledge gained in the field goes a long way.

The landscape history
This is a very extensive subject and does require knowledge of the sort of thing to look for. In other words, one does need to be aware of what particular ground patterns mean in terms of when they evolved and why. (But some extra knowledge is required to obtain the

deeper uses from a map discussed in this chapter anyway.)

A map can show town and village plans and point to their probable development over time; the patterns of roads; the way in which a valley has been drained by ditches; the shape of woodlands; the distribution of settlements and so on. Only in recent times has it been possible to alter the landscape with minimal regard for what was already there – and even motorways have to take account of pre-existing landscape features to some extent. As a result, many of the patterns on a map have remained as fresh land uses are fitted in around the old ones in order to achieve progress with a minimum of unnecessary change – for there comes a point when so much work is involved in making progress that the returns are not worth the effort. This means that the framework of the landscape is still greatly intact, and when you look at a map, you are seeing patterns that are often very old – thousands of years old in cases. It is rather like a room in which the walls are still in the same place, but where there have been several changes of furniture over the years. This is why, to those interested in landscape history, the map is as indispensable as a pair of walking-boots.

Here and there in the book I have tried to show how the map can be used to point to a landscape's past.

Dry valleys

One of the most distinctive features of chalk landscape is the dry valley. It is found in many areas of the North and South Downs and possesses the characteristics of a normal valley except that it has no river in the bottom.

No one is sure how dry valleys were formed, but one likely theory is as follows. Although the ice sheets of the Ice Age did not extend to the region south of London, their influence was felt in those areas close to the ice limit. It would seem likely either that this had the effect of raising the water table (caused by the wetter climate) or that it was cold enough to freeze the ground water and seal the rock. Either way, the result was to render the normally pervious chalk of the Downs impervious and so allow water to flow over them instead of soaking in as it does normally. In the coldest times there might have been no flowing water, but in the periods when the climate was less severe, there would have been, and this is when the valleys were most likely cut.

There are many dry gaps cutting right through the Downs. These serve as valuable transport corridors such as the one carrying the A24 between Washington and Worthing in Sussex. Often, when you look at a map, the contour lines of a whole dry drainage basin can be made out, complete with tributary valleys draining into the main valley.

Later erosion has often blurred the shape of dry valleys. For example, many have lost the 'V' shape in the valley bottom. The reason for this is that, over the centuries since their formation, soil and other material has washed from the sides into the bottom and slowly filled it to form a level, flat area in the valley floor. Often you will see quite large rocks that have rolled into the bottom. Also, the grass there can be much more vivid than that on the valley sides as a result of the soil being enriched by the run-off into the bottom.

When walking between Tottington Barn and the Devil's Dyke, the route crosses a very clear windgap (GR 242109). Seen from below, on the outward section of the round trip, the gap appears as a 'nick' in the scarp. A pylon has been stuck right in the middle of the gap, so it is difficult to mistake. Once on the scarp top, you can actually stand in the 'nick' and, looking southwards, will see that you are at the top end of a dry valley. All that has happened is that erosion has cut the scarp line back past the head of the dry valley — it once would have been further north. Look at the map, and the contour lines will tell the story.

4

East Kent

This section of the walk covers that part of the Kent Downs between Dover on the Channel coast and the village of Detling, near Maidstone. For those proceeding in one direction, this section is divided up into four days walking. These are:

Walk 1   Dover to Lyminge.
Walk 2   Lyminge to Wye.
Walk 3   Wye to Charing.
Walk 4   Charing to Detling.

Those wishing to undertake the walk in round-trips or wanting to return to the starting-point can use the following divisions:

Walk 1   Dover to Lyminge. This is not a round-trip, but it is planned so that a return to Dover is feasible on public transport.
Walk 2   Lyminge as a base for a round-trip travelling westwards to include Brabourne.
Walk 3   Based on Wye, an eastwards circular walk taking in Brabourne.
Walk 4   Wye as the base for a westwards walk to include Charing.

The maps needed for the East Kent walks are:
OS Maps: 179 Canterbury and East Kent; 189 Ashford and Romney Marsh; 188 Maidstone and The Weald of Kent.

An area beginning on the Channel coast and then striking inland along the line of the North Downs. Once it leaves the populous coast and turns inland, the walking is through quiet Kent countryside on generally little-used paths.

There are explorations of the dip slope behind the Downs scarp, along the top of the scarp and out onto the Weald. There are many excellent viewpoints and several places of particular interest.

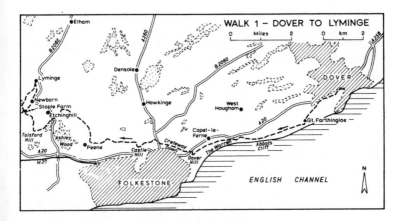

1st Walk: Dover to Lyminge
Total distance: 15 miles
OS map: 179 Canterbury and East Kent

Natural features
Of the natural features on this coast, two things are of particular interest. Firstly, it will be noticed how, over much of the distance between Dover and Folkestone, the cliff top is tilted upwards towards the seaward edge. The reason for this is that chalk tends to lie in a series of gentle 'swells' or smooth hillocks – this relief is to be seen

all over chalk country. What has happened on the cliffs is that one of the 'hillocks' coincides with the point reached by erosion of the coast. The erosion has cut back past the crest of the hillock and leaves the remnant of one slope pointing up into the sky.

Another noticeable landform is the extensive area of grown-over hummocks at the base of the cliffs below Capel-le-Ferne, known as 'The Warren'. What happened here was a landslide, with a chalk layer slipping over the underlying clay and tumbling to the foot of the cliffs.

It would seem best to begin the walk at a point easily located on the 1:50,000 map. On the western side of Dover there is a dual carriageway linking two roundabouts. This is York Road (GR 318414). Having reached York Road, go up Durham Hill, which joins York Road about half way between the two roundabouts.

Once on Durham Hill, follow the road uphill beyond the limits of the built-up area. After about half a mile the road bends sharp left and a No Through Road goes off straight ahead. Take this road.

In a short distance the way is barred by gates and a massive ditch. This immense brick-lined ditch now forms a useful guide to the route as we branch right from the gates and set off on the path along the line of the ditch.

Stay on this path as it takes us gradually away from the ditch and winds around the hillside to give views ahead down the dry valley that carries the Folkestone road.

Note: There are a number of paths in this area. The clearest one is lower down the hillside and in full view below. This is, in fact, the right of way shown on the map. However, this appears to be an area of publicly used land, and the views are better from our rough, unofficial hilltop path. There are views back across Dover.

The path skirts around below the Citadel and then forks; bear right here. The English Channel comes into view on the left, with the French coast very clear in good weather.

On coming to a concrete road, go right, then immediately left to rejoin the path. This is now the path marked on the OS map. Stay with this path, ignoring those to the left and right a little further on. The path performs a gradual descent down the hillside and widens to a track for a short distance. Just above a war-time structure, the path narrows again. At this point leave the path and branch right for a short distance to a fence, using a vague path.

Go over the fence, using the stepping-bar provided, and set a course towards the distinctive hump of downland ahead. This is Great Farthingloe.

This diagonal course leads to another fence with a similar stepping-bar. The area of scrubby downland is now left behind, and the way ahead is across a field on a diagonal course to a road.

Cross the road and go over the stile opposite and up the side of Great Farthingloe to the top of the hill.

The hilltop is also the top of the sea cliffs and is a fine viewpoint.

Go over the stile on the clifftop and follow the path along to the right. This is the North Downs Way. Now there is a period of straightforward unimpeded walking towards Folkestone. The only possible complication is if the ranges are in use above Abbot's Cliff, in which case it is necessary to divert as indicated by the concrete plinths in this area.

There are some rather unsightly structures at the base of the cliffs between Folkestone and Dover. But nothing can detract from the beauty of the Channel on a fine day, its shipping lanes alive with traffic, and the French coast rearing out of the blue haze to the south.

But although the cliffs may be spoilt in places, they are full of interest — natural and man-made. Just after passing the firing-ranges, the path widens to a track and heads towards the A20 Dover-Folkestone road. Follow it to within 50 yards of the road, then go left over a stile marked with a North Downs Way plinth. (The diversion around the firing-range rejoins at this point.) Now continue on along the cliffs again past Capel-le-Ferne and above the Warren to Dover Hill. Here the view is of great interest, for miles away to the south-west, across Folkestone lying beneath our feet, and beyond the great levels of Romney Marsh, are the eastern limits of the South Downs, with Beachy Head a clear 'step' between land and sea. We shall be standing there at the end of the walk, having crossed Kent, Surrey and Sussex on the way.

From Dover Hill the path turns inland. There is a North Downs Way post on the hilltop. Follow this to the right, and the path meets the A20. Go across the A20 and down the minor road opposite, then immediately left over a stile in the left-hand fence (this is opposite a house on the right-hand side of the minor road). Now follow the fence along to the right through the field. Continue on past the triangulation pillar. Here there is a view along the downland scarp to Summerhouse Hill.

At the far end of the field is a stile in the right-hand fence. Go over it to the road on the other side, and then go left across the road junction at this point. Go over the stile on the far side and continue ahead, following the right-hand fence.

Folkestone is now clearly spread out below to the left, and although we are glad that this is one of the few times when urban sprawl intrudes on the landscape on the walk to East Sussex, it does offer an interesting panorama of a town.

Continue along Creteway Down to the next stile, go over it and then go left down the road to meet the A260. Go over the A260 to the junction of 'Crete Road West'. Then go immediately left over a stile and follow the right-hand fence along until you come to the next stile, which is in the fence on the right. Do not go over this stile, but use it as an indicator to bear left away from it. Head across to the crest of the scarp ahead. Once at the crest, follow it along to Castle Hill.

Descend the northern side of Castle Hill to a stile beside a road. Go over the road and up the path opposite where it runs between fences.

Go over the next stile and continue ahead, following the line of the right-hand field boundary. Keep going for almost a mile until reaching a point where the fence strikes downhill and it is impossible to go ahead any further. Here, go over the stile on the right, join the road and turn left. Now proceed downhill along the road.

Go straight on at the next road junction, and bear right at the second road junction. After this second junction the road climbs uphill, returning to the top of the Downs again. The views are now wide-ranging and wholly rural, with Folkestone left behind.

About half a mile after the second road junction there is a small wood on the left. Here, take the second opening on the left – this is a track marked by a North Downs Way plinth.

Continue on this path until coming to a stile on the left. Go over this and follow the right-hand hedge along. Continue in this manner over a further two stiles.

In the third field keep following the right-hand fence all the way around the top of a coombe and then downhill, using the fence as a guide.

At the bottom of the hill there is a stile. Go over it and across the field ahead to a disused railway arch. On the far side of the arch there is a woodland path. Go right here.

Go straight ahead at the edge of the wood, bearing right just below the house at the far side of the field in order to find the stile at the top of the hill. Looking back from here, there is a fairly good view of the series of coombes we have recently been travelling along.

Go right in the lane beyond the stile, and then right upon meeting the B2065. Once on the B2065, go first left up a track. Go along the right-hand fence and then through the woods on a clear path. Go right at the stile on the far side of the woods and stay on the path towards the massive Telecom mast on the hilltop. Cross two stiles beside the mast and follow the perimeter fence ahead to a third stile. Do not cross this stile; turn right in front of it.

Cross the next stile you meet, and then go left along the perimeter fence of the second, smaller, mast. Where the perimeter fence ends, continue on down the hill beside the left-hand field boundary.

Note: The path down from the hilltop is a right of way unshown on the OS. An alternative is the marked path which offers a more direct way to Lyminge. If time is pressing, this is the one to use. However, the alternative longer way gives better views across the Weald and of the classic piece of downland landscape on the side of Tolsford Hill.

On meeting the road at Staple Farm, go right. Go straight ahead at the road junction at New Barn. Pass a house on the left, and go through the second gate on the left.

Now follow the left-hand field boundary ahead and then around to the right along the edge of the field. The path eventually becomes a green lane for a short section before entering a field on the edge of Lyminge. Follow the right-hand fence until coming to a gate on the right. Take this path and it emerges in the village of Lyminge.

Lyminge

Accommodation: Bed and Breakfast is available here. However, its chief value as a staging post on the walk is that, if there are problems in finding a place to stay, it is a simple matter of taking a bus into Dover/Folkestone or the other way to Canterbury, where there is plenty available.

Public transport: Buses to Dover/Folkestone and Canterbury. It is possible to park at Dover, therefore, if a car-owner, and walk to Lyminge, catching a bus back to the car at the day's end.

Parking: There is a free car-park at Lyminge.

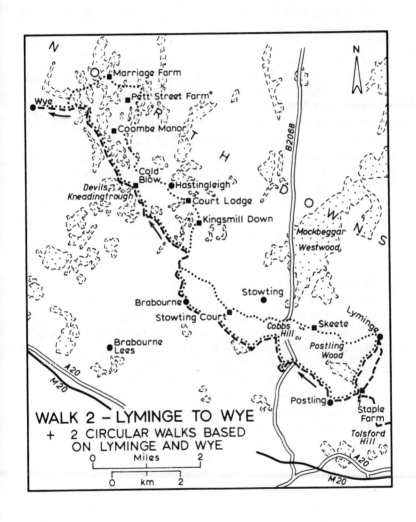

WALK 2 – LYMINGE TO WYE
+ 2 CIRCULAR WALKS BASED
ON LYMINGE AND WYE

2nd Walk: Lyminge to Wye
Total distance: 12 miles
OS maps: 179 Canterbury and East Kent or 189 Ashford
and Romney Marsh

Wye Downs and chalk grassland in general
Wye Downs National Nature Reserve has been
established to protect examples of chalk habitats —
particularly the grassland found in the area. During the
course of the walks along the North and South Downs
many similar sites of conserved chalk grassland will be
encountered. Why, then, is chalk grassland so special?
How did it develop? And, finally, what threatens it that
requires it to be protected?

Chalk grassland is important because it is a wildlife
habitat found only on chalk hills, giving rise to a distinctive
and now comparatively rare flora and fauna. It is an
exceptionally rich and diverse habitat. On Castle Hill
National Nature Reserve on the South Downs near
Brighton some areas of the grassland have thirty different
plant species in a square metre of land. Supported by the
unique flora is a distinctive fauna, of which the most
popularly known are the famous blue butterflies which
depend upon the downland plants.

Chalk grassland developed entirely as a result of
human action. Essentially this involved the clearance of
the native forest from the Downs and the introduction of
livestock farming. We know that chalk grassland is not a
natural condition because full-sized trees grow on the
Downs in areas where it occurs, proving that the land will
support woodland. Left to itself, the downland does in fact
revert to scrub and then woodland. So the delicate
balance by which downland grass is maintained depends
upon grazing to keep out the scrub. This was managed for
many centuries by the grazing of vast downland sheep
flocks and, in pre-myxomatosis days, by rabbits. Chalk

grassland, then, was an accidental result of a particular farming policy. As long as the farming policy persisted, the delicate habitat was maintained. This century the means of farming the Downs has changed dramatically. Basically it is the change in farming methods, particularly during and since the last war, that threatens chalk grassland.

There have been two main causes of the loss of the grassland. Firstly, the ploughing up of the land to plant arable crops. You can easily see the scale of this destruction, for the arable fields stretch for massive distances along the dip slopes of the Downs. Equally, although many areas of the chalk hills do have grass on them, this is often a deliberately seeded single species, sown in place of the downland grass to give a higher yield of animal feed per acre. Biologically it is sterile.

The other way in which chalk grassland is vanishing is by neglect. On those slopes too steep to plough — particularly the steep scarp slopes — the chalk grassland remains but is reverting to scrub. Few areas seem to be grazed now. Hence we have reserves in a few isolated places where deliberate management keeps the grassland open.

Of course, downland grass was never found all over the North and South Downs. On the clay coverings of much of West Sussex, Surrey and Kent woodland has always been widespread, and where cleared the soils would be unlikely to give rise to such grassland. Chalk grassland was very widespread in Sussex east of the Adur — and it is here that the most extensive remaining stretches are to be found almost all along the neglected scarp slope and in some broad sweeps of dip slope. In Kent it is now largely confined to the scarp slope between Folkestone and Wye, and in Surrey the most extensive length is between Reigate and Dorking. You will find numerous pockets of chalk grassland on the walks, the majority of those in Kent and Surrey fighting a losing battle against scrub invasion

– in some localities management is in operation to reverse the trend.

Stage 1: Lyminge to Brabourne

The starting-point of the walk is the Coach and Horses public house in Lyminge. From here go down the High Street. Follow this road until it bends sharp right. At this point go left through a wooden gate behind a barrier of metal railings. This is a bridlepath, though it is unmarked. Follow the right-hand fence uphill across the field.

At the top of the field you meet a stile, go over it and go right along the right-hand hedgerow.

Note: Do not follow the clearer path ahead at this stile.

From here are views across a mixed rolling farmland on the dip slope of the Downs.

Follow the field boundary all the way to the next field. Then cross the fence and continue ahead beside the right-hand fence to a road. Go across the road and over the stile in the hedge opposite. Then go up the field along the right-hand fence past Postling Wood. Reaching the brow of the hill beside Postling Wood, the sea comes into view and the familiar distant bulk of Dungeness power station, a constant reference point throughout the walks in East Kent.

On meeting a fence beside the wood, turn left and follow it downhill, crossing a stile on the way, until coming to the road at Staple Farm. Go right here and follow the road into Postling.

Turn right in Postling, go past the church, and you will come to a footpath on the right marked by a stone plinth. Go over the stile here and go up the hill along the right-hand hedge. Continue along the hilltop, passing a stile on the right, and follow the right-hand fence along the crest of the Downs scarp around to the left.

Here the indented scarp is small-scale and intimate but with wide views beyond over a fine countryside to the south-west. This is real downland walking, unimpeded by fence or stile with extensive grassland on the slope saved by its inaccessibility to machines. Proceed in this manner for about a mile.

The next stile encountered is marked with an acorn waymark. Go over this stile and keep to the right-hand side of the field whilst going straight ahead. Continue on the same heading when the hedgerow on the right ends. There are now distant views ahead along the almost wholly cultivated slopes of the North Downs.

Go left at the B2068 and follow the road downhill to the first road junction. Now go right and proceed down this lane for about mile to the next road junction. Then go left, following the signpost towards Monk's Horton and Sellindge.

Go down the road until about 200 yards beyond Horton Court and then cross the first stile on the right. Bear left across the field to the next stile. Now follow the edge of the woods ahead until meeting another stile. Cross it and go right, through a gate and across a field towards a group of farm buildings.

There is a lane at these buildings. Go left here and follow it to a road junction. Go over a stile in the fence opposite. Now bear right across the field to its far corner. Go over the stile here, and go along the right-hand hedgerow towards a line of pylons.

Cross the next stile and a footbridge, then follow a line of yellow-topped posts ahead across the field. Ignore the waymarked footpath that is crossed before reaching the pylons. Follow the posts across a ditch into the next field and along a hedge on the right. This comes to a gap, enabling access to Brabourne churchyard.

Leave the churchyard by the front gate. Go left on the road and proceed as far as the Five Bells. By a happy coincidence this is roughly the half-way point of the day's walk. Food, and of course drink, is available here.

Go right at the road junction beside the pub and walk as far as the next junction, turn left, then first right. This last turn is onto a road that climbs up the scarp of the Downs.

Stage 2: Brabourne to Wye

Continue up this road over the crest of the Downs, where there are extensive views, and on behind the crest onto the dip slope. Take the first track on the left.

* The track goes clearly around the edge of the field and then continues further on between hedges.

Go left when you come to a road, and walk to the next road junction, where you should go right. Follow this road for some way until coming to a path on the left marked by a North Downs Way plinth. Go over the stile here and across the field. On the far side of the field are two stiles beside each other. Cross the right-hand one and follow the fence ahead to Cold Blow. From here the route is well waymarked and there are sufficient stiles to keep on the route even though the paths themselves may not be especially clear.

You will come to a point where the path diverts around a high chain-link fence. Once past this the small fields around Cold Blow are left behind, and the route is along the crest of the open Downs. The path is marked at intervals by posts all the way to the distinctive Devil's Kneadingtrough.

At the Devil's Kneadingtrough, branch off to the right, following the waymarking posts to a stile. Cross the stile and go over the road to a No Through Road opposite. At the junction of the No Through Road, go left through a gate and on to a second gate.

Now follow the right-hand fence along the top of the Downs for about a mile of straightforward, unimpeded walking, with Wye in view below and ahead. Stay on the hilltop until the way is blocked by a wood. At this point go right over a stile, and walk beside the woods to a road. Go left on the road, then first left over a stile and through the woods. Once out of the woods, the route goes down through a field on a clear path to a road. Cross the road and take the track opposite through Wye College fields all the way into Wye itself.

Circular walk based on Lyminge
Total distance: 11 miles
The furthest extent of this walk is Brabourne. From Brabourne, or rather just beyond it, the return part of the walk begins. Therefore for the outward part of the circular walk, read Stage 1 of the Lyminge to Wye walk in its entirety.

Stage 2: Return route to Lyminge
Once on the road, go uphill until it bends to the left. At this point a track goes off ahead on the bend. Take this track and go through a gate.

Where the track forks, keep to the lower, right-hand fork. Continue on through a gate and below a wood. The path comes out at a road, where you should go straight across onto the opposite side.

At the next road you meet, go left. Go straight on at the next three road junctions. After passing Water Farm (named on its gate), walk for some way uphill to the second footpath on the left past the farm. This is marked by a North Downs Way plinth for confirmation.

This path runs for 100 yards before meeting a road. Cross the road and go over the stile on the other side. Now go uphill beside the right-hand hedge, which then becomes a fence, higher up Cobb's Hill.

Go over the stiles at the top of the hill, continuing ahead along the left-hand fence. At the next stile go left and over a second stile. Here the North Downs Way is left behind because it goes straight ahead at this point and back to Postling.

Once over the second stile, go right and go in a diagonal to the bottom corner of the field where there is a stile. Go straight across the B2068 and down a track opposite. Follow the track to Skeete where it becomes a road. Now walk along this road for half a mile until you come to the first house on the left. Fifty yards beyond here on the right go through a gate and in a diagonal across the field to a stile.

At this stile go over it and turn right through a gateway. Then go immediately left along the edge of a garden to another stile. Cross this and follow the left-hand fence ahead through a field to a road.

Go over the road and up a stepped path on the other side, over a stile at the top of the bank and across a field to another stile clearly visible ahead. Proceed in a diagonal across the next field with Lyminge now in view. Once coming to the road at the edge of Lyminge, go right to get back into the village.

Circular walk based on Wye (eastwards)
Total distance: 11 miles
The round-trip going eastwards from Wye passes close to Brabourne at its furthest point, meeting the furthest extent of the previous circular walk out from Lyminge.

Leave Wye by going past the main College entrance and then first left down Olantigh Road. Go down Olantigh Road past the College laboratories, then first right up a road to the College fields, which then becomes a track.

When the track meets a road, turn left and walk past a house on the right. Then go over a stile on the right and cross a field to its top left-hand corner where there is another stile.

Cross the stile and go through a stand of trees to a road. Cross the road and walk along the path on the other side of the edge of the woods. Here there are views northwards across the rolling chalk country of the Downs dip slope.

At the edge of the woods, turn right and walk along a

track to the next field. In this next field go in a diagonal to the top left-hand corner, cross a fence and follow a clear path through the woods.

On the far side of the woods cross a stile and proceed ahead. The path itself is invisible here, but once on the brow of the hill ahead the route is clear because you can set a line for a gap in the woods in front.

Having reached the gap, walk ahead through a gate and go a further 50 yards on to another path by a large ash tree. Turn right here.

Carry on past Marriage Farm and out across the dry valley bottom beyond to the track on the far side. Cross the track and go ahead through a belt of woodland on the valley side. On the far side of the trees, go straight ahead across a field and drop down to a farm road. Again, there is little or no evidence of the paths on the ground in this area.

Cross the stile on the far side of the farm road and walk straight across a field to another stile. From here walk ahead as far as the nearest corner of a belt of woodland. Once there, go 50 yards up the side of the wood until you reach a point where there is a stile on the left. This shows the line of the footpath you want, so go right here and head across the field around the contour of the hillside.

At the stile on the far side of the field above Pett Street Farm, proceed ahead along the edge of the wood to a gate. Go through the gate and keep following the edge of the wood. Do not go uphill at any time. Maintain a clear path along the edge of woodland, walking the length of the dry valley until near Coombe Manor, which is in clear view over to the right.

At this point you will come to a gate. Go through this and onto a second gate. Once through the second gate, turn left and follow the hedge along. When you meet a fence at the furthest end of the hedge, go left, through the hedge and up the field on the other side until meeting a stile in the right-hand fence.

Note: The paths are invisible here on the ground. When I walked the area, there had been some waymarking with yellow arrows on gates and fences. To the best of my knowledge I have described where the rights of way actually go.

Go over the stile and proceed on a path through the trees to a gate and then go on ahead across a field. Go to the top left-hand corner of the field, pass a small wood and meet a track. Go left on the track and follow it to a crossroads. Go left at the crossroads. At the second crossroads you meet, walk ahead into the village of Hastingleigh.

There is a pub in Hastingleigh, if it is lunchtime when you reach here. Since it is the only village visited on the walk, it might be best to make it lunchtime!

In the village, take the first road on the right, which is signposted to Hastingleigh Church and South Hill. Walk several hundred yards down this road and take the first footpath on the left, which is marked by a concrete plinth.

Keep to the left-hand hedge on this path, and a stile is met. Go over it, and walk along beside the right-hand hedge. When the hedge bends sharp right, continue ahead in a diagonal across the field to a stile at the bottom corner. Maintain the same direction across the next field to Court Lodge.

At Court Lodge go across the road and turn right up past the church to a gate. Go through the gate and go immediately left and follow the line of the churchyard fence along. This brings you to a stile. Go over and follow a broad, though overgrown, path between trees. It is passable. At the far end of this path is a stile. Go over and straight ahead up a hill to a gateway. Go through the gate and maintain the same direction over a second field.

When you come to a road, turn right and follow it for a mile to a track on the right, marked by a North Downs waymarker. From here we are on the return part of the walk. For this stage refer to Stage 2 of the Lyminge to

Wye walk (from the paragraph marked by an asterisk onwards).

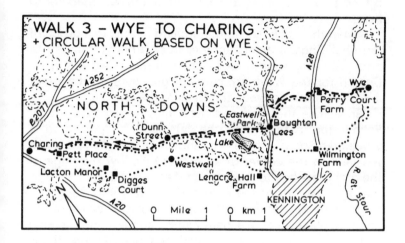

3rd Walk: Wye to Charing
Total distance: 8 miles
OS map: 189 Ashford and Romney Marsh

Wye
Accommodation: This is sparse at Wye. However, this is no problem because it is easy to reach Canterbury or Ashford.
Public transport: There are buses and a rail service to both Ashford and Canterbury.
Parking: There is a free car-park at Wye.

Leave Wye at its western side, crossing the Great Stour and the level-crossing just beyond it. Once over the railway, go left at the road junction. Follow the road to the limit of the houses, then take the first footpath on the right which is waymarked as the North Downs Way. Now follow the line of stiles ahead, visible clearly for the next three fields.

On entering the fourth field, follow the hedgerow, turning right where the hedgerow ends, then left along the edge of the orchard. There are acorn waymarkers to help.

When the track beside the orchard comes to a group of farm buildings, it meets another track running from left to right. Go very slightly right, then immediately left here. Search for the waymark here for guidance on the exact line of the path between the trees to the road.

Go across the road and over the stile on its far side. Follow the path beside the left-hand hedgerow to a waymarker post, where you should turn right and cross the field to the corner of an orchard. Follow the edge of the orchard along to the left and then around the corner to the right. Go left at the road and follow it into Boughton Lees. The walk between Wye and Boughton Lees is rather commonplace stuff. The heavy soils can be murder to slog over in the wet. My boots weighed about three times more after negotiating them. However, from there on things get rapidly better — in terms of both interest and appearance.

Go through Boughton Lees to the road junction at the far side of the village green. Now take the waymarked path on the right. Once in the field, bear left across it towards an avenue of trees where there is a gate in the fence. Cross the estate road and take the gate on the other side. Then strike up across the field to the fence on the skyline. When at the fence, follow it along to the right. Here there is a glimpse of Eastwell Park over to the right.

Continue on past a footpath junction on the left until you come to a road, where you should go ahead down an avenue with the picturesque Eastwell Park lake down to the left.

Just after passing the lake, there is an estate road junction. Go straight on here, over a stile and across the field beyond it to the next stile. On reaching the wood, continue straight on along its edge, turning right at the first waymark signpost. After 100 yards you meet a track. Turn left here. It is now a simple matter of following the track until reaching the first group of farm buildings, met after about two-thirds of a mile.

At this point, just before drawing level with a barn, there is a stile on the left. Go over it and on to a second stile. Look back at the second stile and there is a 'surprise view' all the way to Dungeness. At the road junction beyond this stile, go straight on. As the road climbs the lower part of the Downs, there are views across a thickly wooded farmscape.

At the next fork in the road, bear right. Pass the road junction on the left just beyond and proceed ahead on the signposted Pilgrims' Way, a very clear track. Follow this for a mile until meeting a road serving a working quarry. Go left here and walk until past Burnt House Farm. Past the farm is a bridlepath on the left. Do not take this, but take instead the footpath at this point which is marked by a stile to one side of the bridlepath entrance. Take a diagonal path across two fields (the actual path is invisible on the ground) to the furthest corner of the wall behind Pett Place, where you meet a road. Go left at the road and then turn right at the next road junction. Now proceed to Charing.

Circular walk based on Wye (westwards)
Total distance: 16 miles

Open fields
Near the Great Stour south of Wye it is obvious how 'open' the landscape is. This is in marked contrast to the smaller-scale hedgerowed fieldscapes we have just been walking through. There are a number of areas like this seen on the walks, notably in places along the foot of the Kent Downs and the Sussex Downs. They should not be confused with the open fieldscapes produced by the

reclamation of marshland.

These 'open fields' are remainders from an earlier period of farming, and date to the Saxon period or may be older in cases. The open-field system worked by dividing up the land into strips, which were grouped together as parcels or 'furlongs'. The open landscape we see today is merely an impression of how the fields would have looked, for the means of landholding and strip cultivation which created the fieldscape have vanished. It is just the lack of hedges that gives the areas away. In some districts a common arable farming system did persist as late as the nineteenth century, for example at Alciston below the Sussex Downs. But in general most of the open fields were enclosed by the fourteenth century, so there were more open fields than the present appearance of the landscapes would suggest. However, in many areas the later hedgerows actually follow the old property boundaries of the open fields, and the straightness and regularity of the field patterns can often indicate this. Certainly a great many square plots were created this way in Kent – as well as the commoner rectangular fields.

However, the open-field system was never widespread in the South East (whereas it predominated in the Midlands for a long time). The main reason it did not occur widely was that the soils of the region vary over a small area, and the parishes tended to become 'long and thin', stretching from the Downs to the inner Weald – taking in a range of farmland types for each community. The open fields at the foot of the Downs were the main ploughlands – generally they still are, as at Wye – whilst the Downs and inner Weald were best suited to pasture or woodland management in the Weald forest. So open-field farming was suited to the arable lands at the Downs foot, but largely unsuited to other areas of the South East.

The furthest point reached on this walk out from Wye is Charing, which serves as an excellent lunch stop, with pubs etc.

For the outward part of the journey, read the Wye to Charing walk. The return trip from Charing is as follows.

Stage 2: Return walk to Wye

Leave Charing by way of the road upon which you entered the village. Proceed all the way back to the road junction by Pett Place. Here, go straight on past the front of Pett Place.

Although the return walk uses roads all the way back as far as Boughton Lees, they are all very quiet Kent lanes between deep hedgerows. I met only two cars on the summer's afternoon on which I walked it, and it is a far more pleasant route than thrashing around for extinct footpaths in wet wheatfields and waterlogged ploughland.

Go left at the next road junction, and bear around to the left at the second. At the third road junction, take the left turning to Westwell.

At Westwell go straight ahead on the road past the Wheel Inn. The road is signposted for Wye, Boughton Lees and Kennington. Walk on past the church and leave the village. Go straight on at the next junction towards Kennington and Eastwell. Go straight on at the next road junction. From here there are views across to Wye Downs with the Crown chalk effigy particularly clear in the hillside. Now walk the remaining mile to the A251. Go left at the A251 past the entrance to Eastwell Park.

Follow the A251 for about half a mile on the pavement. After half a mile you will pass a house on the left. Two hundred yards beyond here, on the opposite side of the road, is a gap in the hedge. The path is invisible on the ground, and it is unsignposted, so it can be tricky to locate. However, it is on the map, so if in doubt trust to following a straight line towards Wilmington Farm which is visible from the A251, although you will lose sight of it part-way across the field. Take a compass bearing to do the job properly.

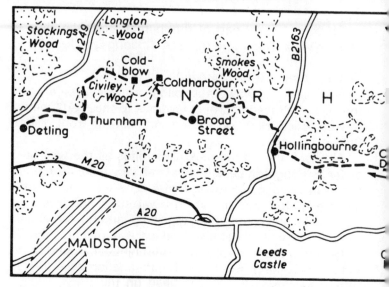

Nearing Wilmington Farm, the 'path' becomes a track which is to be followed to the A28.

Go right at the A28, then immediately left on a track out towards the quiet fields beside the Great Stour, an area with that tangible loneliness so common in the flat lands beside lowland rivers.

In this area of the walk there is likely to be some confusion. The OS map shows the track ending short of the Ashford/Wye railway line. In fact it goes all the way to the railway line. This makes the location of the path off to the left difficult, especially since the path itself is indistinct on the ground.

To find the path, follow these instructions. Leave the track to cross the field and head for the footbridge over a ditch on its far side (just visible from the track). Use the positions of the wood to the right of the track and the ditches marked on the map to locate the path.

Once at the footbridge, go straight ahead to the railway embankment, then turn left and walk along beside the

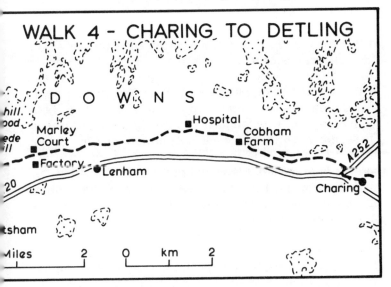

embankment as far as a level crossing. Go over the crossing.

Go immediately left once over the crossing, across a fence and in a diagonal over a field towards a bridge over the Great Stour.

4th Walk: Charing to Detling
Total Distance: 14 miles
OS Maps 189 Ashford and Romney Marsh; 188 Maidstone and The Weald of Kent.

Charing
Accommodation: This is available in Charing, including Bed and Breakfast.
Public transport: Buses to Maidstone, Ashford and Canterbury railway station with links to Maidstone, Ashford, Wye and Canterbury.
Parking: There is a free car-park at Charing.

Coverts

In this area, and several other places seen on the walks, there are stands of trees out in the fields. Generally these are very small woods, covering just a few acres, and usually consist of mature trees, with a thick undergrowth, surrounded by perimeter hedge. They are often fairly regular in plan – rectangular or roughly circular perhaps. These are coverts and were deliberately planted as fox refuges to encourage them to remain on land on which hunting is practised. Many still perform this function, but many have ceased to have a use in areas where hunting no longer takes place. Many of the coverts are used as pheasant cover on shoots.

Leave Charing down School Road, which is a turning off the main street. Walk as far as the A20/A252 roundabout, where you should go right and follow the A252 for a short distance on the left-hand pavement. Take the first footpath on the left you come to; it is marked by a concrete plinth.

Now walk in a diagonal across two fields to intercept the Pilgrims' Way, which is clearly visible as a line of trees following the lower contours of the Downs. Step over the fence to join the Trackway (if you manage to meet the fence at the correct place, it is lower at this point to facilitate access). Go left on the Pilgrims' Way and continue for about half a mile.

Go right on meeting a road, then first left through a gate to rejoin the Trackway. Now walk for about a mile to Cobham Farm. Here you meet another track serving the farm, where it is necessary to turn right and then left past the barns to proceed along a clear path between hedges. Keep going for about a mile as far as a road below a hospital. Cross the road and walk ahead as far as another road. Go straight ahead along the road, until meeting a sharp left-hand bend. At this point the Trackway goes off ahead, behind a line of white railings on the bend. Go down the Trackway along an enclosed section, until it crosses a large open pasture above Lenham. Upon meeting a minor road, walk straight ahead until meeting a larger road. At this point it is possible to divert into Lenham.

If not diverting into Lenham, turn right at the road past a terrace of houses and then leave the road by the first track on the left. Nearing Harrietsham, you will meet another road. Here, go straight on down the lane. It is enclosed for the most part by high hedgerows. Continue for just over a mile until you come to a crossroads.

Go straight across here, down a minor road. This road eventually gives way to a path. There is now straightforward walking along the Pilgrims' Way, the path following a course between banks and hedges at the foot of the scarp. After some time the path runs within and beside a shaw, through an area of full-timbered hedgerows.

Pass any paths going off to left or right. Simply keep straight on all the way to Hollingbourne.

Nearing Hollingbourne, the North Downs scarp comes into view over to the right, being a well-defined bare slope at this point.

Turn right on the B2163 in Hollingbourne. Walk 50 yards and then take a signposted footpath on the left of the road. This path follows the hedgerow up to a stile and then ascends the downland scarp on a fairly clear path defined by the shorter, worn sward. There are acorn waymarking posts to help here. Walk up the slope as far as a large clump of bushes part way up the hill. Turn left on reaching these bushes and follow the path along the contour around the hillside.

Here the height gives the first long-range views of the day across the thickly wooded Weald, gently undulating on the now-apparent rise of the Greensand ridge. To the West is the distant sweep of the North Downs on the far side of the Medway, where we shall be in two days' walking.

Once around the bend of the hillside, the path strikes uphill to the right, away from the clearer path ahead. Again, there is waymarking to help at this point.

Continue on through the scrub and thickets. It can be confusing in this area because there are many paths, human and animal, weaving in and out of the scrub. The best plan is to keep to roughly the same level and height and follow the scarp around until you come to a stile, sited at a clear junction with another path. This is on the edge of an area of woodland.

Note: This area, at the time of writing, is totally devoid of waymarking. It needs waymarking, for it is easy to go astray here. In all fairness it should be said that most of the North Downs Way and the multitude of lesser-known paths used on the walks are in general very well marked and maintained.

Go over the stile and turn left downhill for a short distance, and then go first right along a fairly clear path for almost a mile through a mixture of woodland and some open fields until meeting a road, where you go left.

Note: In the area between here and Thurnham it was my intention to utilize hilltop paths out to Coldharbour. However, paths shown on the map have been so neglected on the ground that they are invisible. For this reason I used the road between Hucking Hill to near Coldharbour. Anyone wishing to rediscover the hilltop paths and establish their rights may do so – but expect the worst!

Follow the road downhill all the way to the junction at Broad Street, where you should go right. After about half a mile there is a No Through Road on the left with a bridlepath on the right opposite it. Go up the bridlepath and follow it up onto the North Downs scarp. After the path curves around to the left, it forks. At this point go right and follow it up through a belt of woodland to

The North Downs near Folkestone, a view of Castle Hill from
Creteway Down

Looking towards Stowting Hill from Cobb's Hill

Postling: a quiet hamlet in a fold of the North Downs countryside

The Devil's Kneading-Trough is one of the few locations on the Kent Downs that still supports chalk grassland

Heavily wooded farmland: a typical hilltop view of the Kent Weald
from the North Downs

Hollingbourne on the Pilgrims' Way en route to Detling

Thurnham churchyard, a secluded haven in a district of wide open fields

Westhumble: one of Surrey's many peaceful beauty spots

Coldharbour Farm. Then turn left on an unmarked, but visible, path opposite the farmhouse. Follow the hedgerow until coming to a field boundary blocking the route. Cross this and continue straight on along a grassy path between the fields. There is a massive booster station over to the right here.

At the minor road at Coldblow, proceed along it to a road, where you should turn right. Then turn first left down a track. Follow this path ahead through the trees and then along the left-hand boundary of the field beyond to a stile on its far side. Cross the stile and follow the path beyond to a minor road, where you should turn left and follow the road as it bears around to the right on a bend. Keep on along the road until near to a radio mast ahead, at which point there is a track on the right of the road. Exactly opposite this track a path, which we take, heads out across the field towards the far side. This is totally ploughed out on the ground, and as the far side of the field is also out of sight beyond the rise in the land, the line of the path has to be walked on a compass bearing.
Note: In the area of Civiley Wood there have been some changes which can lead to map-reading problems. Chiefly this is because there is now much less woodland remaining than the OS map shows. Also, the lack of clearly defined paths on the ground is a problem.

Once on the far side of the field, follow the eastern edge of a wooded area downhill around the old mound of Thurnham Castle to meet a road. Go left down the road. On meeting a road junction in Thurnham, turn right and follow this road all the way to Detling.

5

Medway

This fairly small division of the walk encompasses those lengths of the North Downs lying to either side of the Medway Gap.

There are two days walking for those going in one direction:

Walk 5   Detling to the Medway Bridge.
Walk 6   Medway Bridge to Wrotham.

There are two days walking for those returning to a base:

Walk 5   Detling to the Medway Bridge. Not a circular walk, but it is possible to return to Detling.
Walk 6   Based on Wrotham. A circular walk eastwards taking in West Halling.

OS maps: 188 Maidstone and The Weald of Kent; 178 The Thames Estuary.

Where the North Downs strike northwards either side of the River Medway, a distinctive area of Kent is created. Between Detling and the Medway Bridge the walk follows the scarp for the most part, dropping down into the valley nearing the Bridge. Between the Bridge and Wrotham there is walking both on the scarp and below it. A great deal is in woodland.

There are some long-range views where the breaks in the woodland allow. The area gives an interesting and somehow compatible mixture of prehistoric monuments and modern industry. It is a varied landscape of wood, farmland, river and distant towns, never close enough to spoil the walk but rather to give it an added dimension. There is something strangely evocative about industry glimpsed from afar within a landscape.

The Medway megaliths

White Horse Stone is an unexciting remnant taken by itself, but it marks our arrival in an area of outstanding prehistoric interest.

In general there is a poverty of prehistoric features on the North Downs – certainly nothing to compare with the Sussex hills. But the big exception is the Medway area where there is a distinctive group of neolithic tombs that makes this one of the most significant archaeological areas in Britain.

Walking the South Downs we shall see long barrows, also constructed at the time of the Medway examples, but the megaliths are of a different type and no doubt indicate another culture or race. The megaliths are 'chambered tombs' with stone-lined interiors (megalith means 'giant stone') which would have formed a passage within a large earthen mound. The mounds are now gone, leaving the stones.

The first encountered, close to each other, are Kit's Coty House and Little Kit's Coty House. The latter is locally called the 'Countless Stone' and is a tumbled mass of fallen stones. However, up the hill is Kit's Coty House, consisting of two standing stones supporting a massive capstone. This remnant is of the central chamber of the barrow – called a 'dolmen'.

But the big fascination is this. Way across the Medway valley in a line from Kit's Coty House is a megalithic tomb of the same type – though better preserved – called the Coldrum Stones. Just to the south of the Coldrum Stones is a set of stones in the same relationship to them as Little Kit's Coty House is to Kit's Coty House. This is significant and speaks of large-scale landscape design with all four interrelated. Local legend even speaks of a sarsen avenue

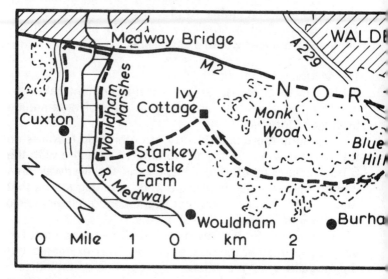

linking the two sides of the valley.

The Coldrum Stones are near Trottiscliffe. Unfortunately half of the hillock on which the barrow stands has since been cut away. What we see now is half the hillock with the majority of the stones fallen but roughly in position. When the earth mound covered these stones, it must have been a massive object.

5th Walk: Detling to the Medway Bridge
Total distance: 11 miles
OS map: 178 The Thames Estuary.

Detling
The main value of Detling as a base is its accessibility by bus from Maidstone. Maidstone is probably the best base for this area of the walk for it has parking and accommodation and is readily accessible by bus and train.

Also, if you wish to return to a base at the end of the

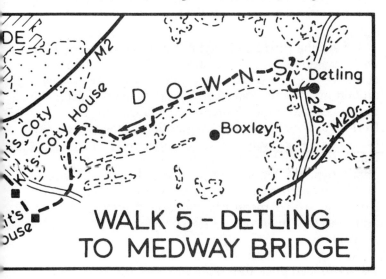

WALK 5 - DETLING
TO MEDWAY BRIDGE

day, it is more straightforward to get back to Maidstone from the Medway Bridge area than Detling.

Leave Detling at the top end of the village, taking the road on the left beside the Cock Horse pub. This road comes out at the A249.

Go straight across the A249 and down the road opposite. Walk until 50 yards beyond the first junction on the left. At this point there is a minor road off to the right, and you should take this up past a quarry until almost on the top of the hill. In this area you pass a path on the right and should then go a further 50 yards until coming to a path on the left. Take this path and follow it along the scarp crest with vast arable fields extending on the dip slope over to the right. The views over to the left are largely hidden by the thick woodland on the scarp slope, although there is an early glimpse over to Maidstone.

Go along this path for over a mile and a quarter, passing any paths on the left, until you come to a road

junction. Go straight ahead here (signposted Walder-
slade).

Where the road bends right at Harp Farm, leave it and
walk straight ahead up a track. As the track peters out,
continue ahead along the left-hand fence and follow it
around into the woodland on the scarp slope. Just inside
the woods, turn right along the woodland path.

Note: I suspect that the configuration of the woods near
Harp Farm has altered since the map was drawn. Also,
you can see that the line of the Trackway actually goes
ahead over the arable land, rather than into the woods.
This is an alternative that rejoins our own route. However,
if its use would mean the damage of crops, it seems
unnecessarily malicious to do so when an alternative is
available.

At the next path junction, which is marked by a
yellow-topped post, turn right and walk uphill to the edge
of the trees. Once there, turn left and follow the woodland
periphery along. There is a point here where a lane is cut
through the woodland to enable the passage of overhead
power lines. This gives excellent views across Maidstone
and to the Downs on the far side of the Medway.

At the next path junction, turn left and follow the path
down through the woods on what becomes a fairly steep
descent. At the foot of the scarp you meet a broad, clear
path. Turn right here. The White Horse Stone is a little
further on, on the right of the path.

As the path becomes a small road, keep straight on
until you meet the A229. Go across the main road and
you will encounter a bridlepath on its other side marked
by a North Downs Way plinth. (Do not take the footpath
50 yards to the left of the bridlepath entrance.) Now you
are in full view of the Medway valley and the factories and
mills of Snodland and New Hythe.

Continue on the path, past a junction on the left, and
you will then meet a road. (Here you can divert a short
distance left down the road to see Little Kit's Coty House,

before returning to this point.) At the road go straight over, then right, up a path signposted to Kit's Coty House. The dolmen is on the left near the top of the hill.

Follow the path up the hill to a road. Now go left and follow the pavement along to the A229. Follow the A229. For the most part you are below the level of the dual carriageway, on the line of the old main road. When the path comes up besides the A229 again, continue on for about 200 yards until you come to a road on the left (Common Road). Go down here, then almost immediately left on a path.

Fifty yards down the path, turn right over a stile. This brings you out on Bluebell Hill, arguably the best viewpoint of the Medway valley.

Bluebell Hill is a picnic area, with car-parking provision on the right-hand hilltop above the path. Once past this parking area, look up to the right for a stile. This is the route away from here, and care should be taken not to walk past this point.

You will meet a road just beyond the stile. Go left here and stay on the road until it ends at Burham Hill Farm. Here it becomes an unmetalled track. Continue on, and where the track forks at a gate to the Keeper's Lodge, bear around to the right.

Over to the right as the walk progresses, there are views of the massive refinery on the Isle of Grain to the north-east and of Rochester to the north-west.

When you come to a point where the track bends sharply to the left, leave it and proceed ahead along a narrow path. A plinth marks this point. Just on from here the path opens out on the hillside to give a striking view ahead of the Medway Bridge.

At the next path junction, leave the North Downs Way and go left downhill to a cottage. Go past the cottage, over the road beyond and onto the track opposite. The massive cement works at Halling are now looming clearly ahead on the far side of the river.

At the next road go straight over and down the track past Starkey Castle Farm. Go through the farmyard and out through the gate beyond. Now follow the grassy track ahead towards the River Medway.

Landscape 'relics'

As you walk through the field towards the Medway embankment, look carefully and you will see a number of depressions in the surface. See the pattern they make and it becomes clear that they are the remnants of old creeks. What has happened is that the former tidal creeks beside the Medway have been cut off from the river and absorbed into the farmland and have been either deliberately earthed in or gradually filled over the years by natural processes. It is worth looking for such signs in any similar area. In some cases the creeks may remain as freshwater pools or still be used as ditches. In others the whole pattern may have been ploughed out – a lot does depend upon the subsequent use of the land.

This is just one example of a remnant of a former landscape feature. Others could be the depressions left in the ground by former, long disused roads, the old ditches and ramparts of hill-forts, the uneven field surface left by a deserted village – anything which is now gone from the landscape and has been superseded by something else but has left a sign that it was once there, however faintly, in the terrain.

At the embankment top, go right and follow it towards the Medway Bridge – a landmark which you have to close your eyes to miss! Near the bridge the embankment path ends. Continue on the track ahead past the moorings and then follow it around to the right away from the river bank. When the track meets a road, go left along the road. Take the last turning off the road before the bridge. Go up onto the bridge and cross it by means of the footway. On the far side of the bridge, go left into Cuxton.

Cuxton
Cuxton has little to offer as a base for walkers. However, it is readily accessible from Maidstone and Rochester by public transport so either of these places can be used in this area.

6th Walk: Medway Bridge to Wrotham
Total distance: 10 miles
OS maps: 178 The Thames Estuary; 188 Maidstone and The Weald of Kent.

Stage 1: Cuxton to Horseholders Wood
Leave Cuxton past the White Hart pub and up the hill beyond towards Halling. When past the White Hart, take the first track on the right that you come to. It is signposted as a footpath to Upper Halling and Bush. Go through the churchyard along the left-hand wall to a gate, where there is a track. Go right here, uphill. At the top end of the track, turn left through some gates and cross the field along the right-hand hedge to a stile. Cross the stile and you are on a clear path between hedges. Continue on into the woods ahead.

At the next crossroads of paths, proceed straight ahead. When you come to a small clearing beneath a line of overhead power cables, the North Downs Way comes in from the right; continue straight ahead along it.

Of interest throughout today's walk is the extensive acreage of traditionally managed deciduous woodland. This is again seen in Surrey and is discussed in detail on p 112-113.

On passing beneath a second line of power lines, there is a path junction, where you should carry on ahead. At a path junction beyond, which is waymarked, turn right along the North Downs Way. A little further on is a crossroads – go ahead here. On reaching the far edge of

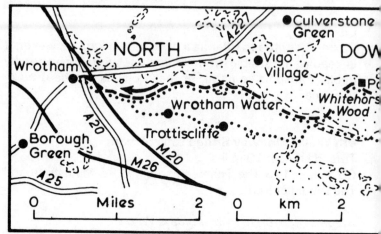

the woods, proceed ahead on a clear path across a field. (Do not turn left on the path at the woodland edge.) Once across the field and at the woods on its far side, continue straight ahead. This area is all a part of Horseholders Wood. Turn right at the next path junction, and then straight on past the next path from the left. About 25 yards from this junction you meet a track, where you should go across and ahead through a field to more woodland on the far side. Once in the woodland you will meet another track, where you go left. Follow this track to a gate, go through it and turn right onto another track. Then turn first left on a path through it and turn right onto another track. Then turn first left on a path through a gap in the hedge. The path then leads clearly across a field to more woodland. There is a junction of paths just behind the line of trees when you have crossed the field.

Stage 2: Horseholders Wood to Wrotham

At this junction walk straight ahead and follow the path to Holly Hill Farm. At the farm the path becomes a metalled road, which you should follow all the way to a car-park on the right. At this point there are good views, over to the

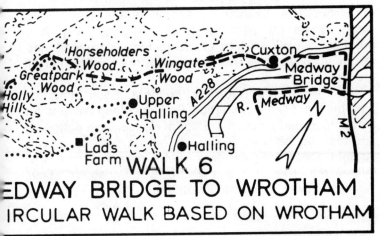

WALK 6
ＥDWAY BRIDGE TO WROTHAM
ＩRCULAR WALK BASED ON WROTHAM

left, of the Medway and the massive quarries below Bluebell Hill. It is one of the few long-distance views obtained today as the walks are generally in thick woodland.

It is the last we shall see of this area before we turn west towards Wrotham. Not without a little regret, for the Medway is a fascinating area of Kent. A mix of fine countryside and industry with a haunting of prehistory.

Go into the car-park and leave by the path at the rear. Stay on the main path through the woods until meeting a road. Turn right at the road and proceed for about half a mile to Poundgate. At Poundgate there is a path on the left. It is clearly marked as a footpath, and there is a stile. This path through Whitehorse Wood is in fact a section of the Weald Way long-distance path, which runs from the Thames Estuary to the English Channel across the heel of England. Half way through the wood there is a path crossroads – go straight ahead here. Now follow the path all the way down to the Pilgrims' Way at the foot of the North Downs scarp.

Note: In this area there are a number of waymarked guided walks associated with Trosley Country Park, but there should be no problem in keeping to the correct path. *Note*: Where the path meets the Pilgrims' Way, it is possible to walk straight ahead to the Coldrum Stones, returning to the Way at this point for the continuation of the walk.

On meeting the Trackway, go right. Soon after, the path becomes a metalled road. Proceed along the road for a mile to a road junction at Pilgrim House. Turn right here and then go left after 200 yards onto a path. Now walk straight ahead long the path until it meets a road. Now follow this road for a mile to a roundabout above Wrotham. Walk down into Wrotham.

Wrotham
Accommodation: This is available in Wrotham.
Public transport: There are bus services to the village. The nearest railway station is at nearby Borough Green.
Parking: There is a free car-park in Wrotham.

Circular walk based on Wrotham, eastwards to West Halling
Total distance: 14 miles
OS map: 188 Maidstone and the Weald of Kent
Leave Wrotham by following the High Street out of the village until opposite some tennis courts, where you should take a path on the right. On coming to a road, go across it and turn left, walking along beside the road. At the roundabout leave by the first road on the right. The steep Downs scarp is now in view on the left as you walk along this road, leaving the Hell of the road intersections behind.

Follow this lane for about three-quarters of a mile, and then turn right at the first road junction. Now walk for 500 yards or so down this road. Take a path on the left. It is unmarked on the ground, but its location can be judged by taking a line from the road to the near end of a belt of trees on the far side of the field. Once you have reached the end of the trees, continue ahead along the left-hand fence line to Wrotham Water in clear view ahead. At Wrotham Water cross a stile and keep on ahead past the buildings to a road. Proceed straight ahead along the road all the way to Trottiscliffe.

At Trottiscliffe turn left up Taylors Lane and then go first right down Green Lane. As the lane ends, go straight ahead on a path through a gate to a church visible ahead. Go through a farm and past the church. Just past a small group of houses, turn left up a path to a stile, then go ahead on a clear path across a field.

On meeting a road, go across it and down a track opposite, giving way in time to a clear path through fields. Coming over a rise, there is a first sight of the industrial chimneys of the Medway. At the next junction of paths turn left.

Note: Here it is possible to divert right to see the Coldrum Stones, returning to this point.

Now follow this path to the Pilgrims' Way at the foot of the scarp and turn right. Stay with the North Downs Way for some distance, following the plinths past three paths going off to the left. At the fourth junction of paths, where a path comes in from the right, bear around to the left. There is a North Downs Way plinth as a confirmation.

At the next path junction (a crossroads) go straight on. Here you leave the North Downs Way, because it goes left at this point.

On meeting a road, go left, then immediately right. Follow this path until meeting a farm track, where you should proceed ahead. Stay on this track, ignoring any paths off. From here one can appreciate the full scale of the quarrying in the Medway gap. At the road, turn right and walk along to Lad's Farm. Continue ahead at the road junction at Lad's Farm. You are some way from the scarp here, and over to the left Crookhorn Wood is situated on a prominent spur of the chalk hills.

Walk right through to the far end of Halling, and turn left up a No Through Road at a road junction by 'The Robin Hood' public house.

Take this road up to the farm and then turn left. Now follow this route to a road. Turn right at the road and follow it for about half a mile to a track on the left at Greatpark Wood. Then turn first right up a path marked by a stone plinth. Now follow this path up beside Greatpark Wood to a path junction after about one third of a mile.

For the return trip from here to Wrotham, read Stage 2 of the Medway Bridge to Wrotham walk.

6

West Kent and Surrey

This section encompasses all of the North Downs between Wrotham and Farnham. It is split into five days' walking:

Walk 7   Wrotham to Westerham.
Walk 8   Westerham to Reigate.
Walk 9   Reigate to Westhumble (Dorking).
Walk 10   Westhumble (Dorking) to Artington.
Walk 11   Artington to Farnham.

There are six days' walking from a base:

Walk 7   Wrotham to Westerham. Not a round-trip. A return to Wrotham is feasible.
Walk 8   Westerham to Reigate. This is not a circular walk, but Westerham can be returned to.
Walk 9   Reigate as the base for a circular walk travelling westwards as far as Box Hill.
Walk 10   Westhumble or Dorking as the base. A circular walk westwards taking in Oaken Grove (north of Gomshall).
Walk 11   Based on Gomshall. A round-trip extending westwards as far as Shalford.
Walk 12   Artington to Farnham. Not a round-trip. A return to Artington is possible.

The following OS maps are needed: 187 Dorking, Reigate and Crawley; 186 Aldershot and Guildford.

The walking in this area takes us close to the outer suburbs of London and the large Surrey towns, yet it is almost entirely in woodland and farmland. It is homely

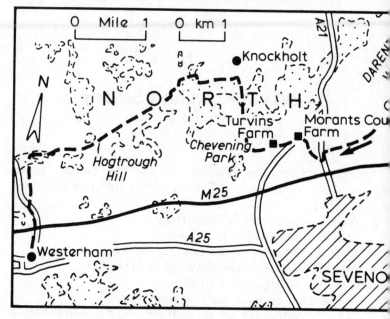

countryside, perhaps a little over-tame in parts, but still with plenty of quiet and unexpected isolation.

There are many fine views, with walks along the scarp, over the dip slope of the North Downs and out onto the Weald. As the route progresses westwards into western Surrey, the walks forsake the chalk in favour of the Greensand running to its south, a gradual transition that is felt under foot and in the surroundings.

7th Walk: Wrotham to Westerham
Total distance: 15 miles
OS maps: 188 Maidstone and the Weald of Kent; 187 Dorking, Reigate and Crawley.
Note: This section of the long-distance walk follows the North Downs Way, and as many of the paths to be used are not shown on the map, it is best to rely on the

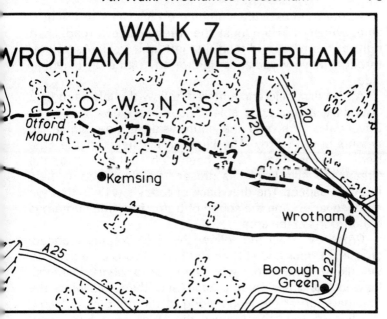

WALK 7
WROTHAM TO WESTERHAM

DOWNS

Otford Mount

M20

A20

●Kemsing

Wrotham●

A25

Borough Green●

A227

excellent waymarking if there is any confusion over the lack of mapped routes.

To leave Wrotham, walk uphill past Wrotham Church and then take the first road on the left (Old London Road). Now proceed until past the primary school, where there are Pilgrims' Way and North Downs Way signs, and go first left. Follow this road until it bends sharp left, and then continue straight ahead on a track at this point. You are now on a hedge-bounded path, slightly elevated with views to the left towards the Greensand hills. Go straight across the first road you meet, onto the continuation of the track opposite. At the second road you come to, turn right and cross a stile which is on the right at the junction with the road. Now go uphill across the fields – the line to take, via the next two stiles, is clearly visible from this first stile. Climbing the scarp, there are views south as far as the Sussex Downs.

At the topmost stile, continue on 50 yards to the next stile, which is in amongst the trees beside a road. Turn right at the road, and then first left up a track. As you go through these woodlands, ignore any paths off to either side.

At the first field encountered, follow the left-hand field boundary along to a stile. There are views across to Sevenoaks here, and the countryside is now similar to neighbouring Surrey. The large arable fields of the East Kent Downs foot have been left behind, and the Greensand hills in places present an almost completely forested aspect. The drawback of today's walk is that we hardly ever escape the sound of traffic from the numerous major roads in the area.

Cross the stile and follow the field boundary ahead, crossing a track and stile *en route*, until you come again to woodland. Enter the woodland for a short distance, leaving the trees over a stile and then following the outside edge of the wood along to the right. Now follow the line of the stiles across the fields to a farm road. Follow this road through a farmyard to a lane. Turn left and go downhill for some distance. Then turn onto the first track on the right.

Turn first right off this track over a stile and follow the left-hand fence along and into some woods. On the far side of the woods, go ahead beside the left-hand line of trees, which then joins a track. As the track meets another field, go left over two stiles through the width of a shaw, and then follow the left-hand field boundary around to the next stile.

Cross the stile and go right, along beside a fence. The path is now along the crest of the North Downs with views over to the south again. At the next stile continue on, across a track on its other side and then along a path across the hillside. This is Whiteleaf Down.

On crossing the next stile, you are back into woodland. When the path divides, take the right-hand (uphill) fork.

Then turn right at the next path junction and follow it uphill all the way to a fence at the edge of the woodland. Go left and follow the fence until the next junction of paths, where you should go around to the right.

When you meet a road, turn left, and then turn right at the next road 50 yards on. After walking 150 yards down this road, go left over a stile and follow a clear line across the fields (via two stiles) to another road. Turn left at the road and follow it to a road junction, where you should go straight ahead and over a stile beside a gate. Cross the field beyond beside the left-hand boundary, then over a stile and through an area of woodland before emerging from the trees and dropping down towards Otford with views opening up ahead of the Darent Valley and the Downs to the west.

Note: I had considered missing out Otford and the messy tangle of roads that has to be negotiated in this area. The idea had been to divert up through the much more pleasing Darent Valley. However, in view of the intended motorway scheme through the valley, and the inevitable degradation that will result, there is probably little point.

When you encounter the minor road near Otford, turn right. Then turn left on joining the A225, and follow it into Otford, where there are a number of pubs to have lunch if wanted.

From the main road roundabout in the centre of Otford, go ahead through the older part of the village. Now walk for almost a mile and take the second road on the left, where there is a North Downs Way plinth and a signpost to Duncton Green. Proceed on down this road past any estate road junctions until the next waymarking plinth, which directs you ahead down a rough-surfaced road.

As the track crosses a railway, it ends. At this point go over a stile and proceed on a clear route across the fields to the A2028. Turn left at the A2028, and then right at the next road junction. Now follow this road across the A21 dual carriageway and then turn first left. Follow this minor road all the way past the North Downs Way path (on the right, at Morants Courts Farm) and on to Turvins Farm. At the bend in the road just beyond Turvins Farm, continue straight ahead onto a clear public footpath. Now keep on to Chevening Church visible ahead.

Enter Chevening Churchyard and go right on a tarmac path, leaving the churchyard through a gate. Then walk ahead up a clear path beside the parkland of Chevening. Stay on this path, passing a stile on the left after almost half a mile. A little further on from here there is a path coming in from the right. Keep straight on, though from here onwards the path is poorly defined, so use the left-hand fence as the guide until reaching the clearer route through an area of woodland.

At the next stile you re-encounter the North Downs Way, where you should go ahead for less than 50 yards along a section of metalled road before going left over a stile. Now proceed through the fields along the left-hand boundary. There are stiles at each hedge you meet. At the third stile look left and you can see down the 'Keyhole Viewpoint' to Chevening House almost a mile away – a classic 'surprise view'.

At the sixth stile turn left through a broad ride cut in a wood, then go around the edge of the wood to a stile. Cross the stile and go left along the left-hand fence on a clear path. When you come to a road, go across and over the stile opposite.

Note: This is a confusing section where waymarking would be a help on the unclear paths.

Follow the left-hand hedge along to a corner of the field and turn right along the hedge until meeting a stile. If on course, there should be a small wood over to the right at this point.

Go over the stile and follow the left-hand hedge all the way around to the next stile, where you continue ahead beside the left-hand fence. Just before meeting a road, turn left over two stiles and then turn right and follow the hedge. You are now running parallel with the road, which is on the other side of the hedge. Keep on going in this manner until you meet a road. Cross the road and the stile opposite, now following the left-hand hedge ahead to the next road, which is also to be crossed. Having crossed it, follow the left-hand hedge ahead.

When you come to waymarks by a stile (this is on Hogtrough Hill, for point of reference), follow their directions up to the right along a fence line to a wood. At the wood, turn left and follow its perimeter to a stile, where you should follow the path beyond around to the right. Now views are regained over to the Greensand hills with Westerham at last in view ahead to the left.

Turn left once across the next stile and follow the right-hand hedge along to yet another stile. Cross this and go ahead through one field, then turn left along the furthest hedge boundary, following the North Downs Way direction post. Then follow a track around to the right as far as a junction with another track, where you go left, downhill. After 150 yards go over a stile on the left and down the field beyond to a clearly visible stile. Once over this, continue through the woods to another stile, where you go right, along a hedge to the next stile on the right. But do not cross this last stile. Instead go left, leaving the North Downs Way. Follow the edge of the field to a road. Cross the road and a stile opposite.

Note: This path is marked at each end but is overgrown in places, though passable. It in fact seems to be a green lane all the way down from the North Downs Way.

Once over the stile, follow the left-hand boundary ahead and through the remnants of a green lane into the second field as far as the A233. Now turn left and follow the main road into Westerham.

Westerham

Accommodation: This is available in Westerham, but if there are problems, it is a fairly short bus ride back to

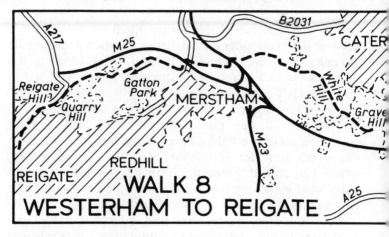

Sevenoaks.

Public transport: There are buses in either direction, to Reigate or Sevenoaks. Those wishing to return to Wrotham can do so by bus via Sevenoaks.

Parking: There is a free car-park at Westerham.

8th Walk: Westerham to Reigate
Total distance: 16 miles
OS map: 187 Dorking, Reigate and Crawley

Countryside close to London
In the distance can be seen the suburbs of south London. They are always near when walking the Surrey Downs, but they are seen only distantly and seldom intrude on the walk. It adds a rather strange dimension to the walk to be in such fine countryside yet to glimpse on occasions the nearness of our largest city as the sunlight picks out a distant tower glinting in the haze or the tide of red roofs rolling beyond sight to central London.

London has a massive influence on the region around it – indeed on the whole of the Britain. However, this

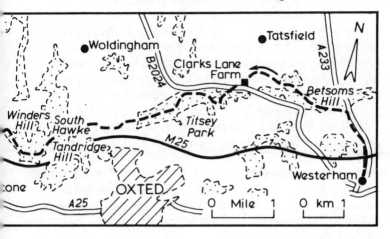

influence is particularly noticeable, in visual terms, in the countryside close to its outer suburbs, with decreasing impact as the distance from London increases – but this is only a very general rule.

The countryside close to London has been described by a number of terms, the most familiar being 'the greenbelt'. Virtually all the time in Surrey we are walking within the London greenbelt, land that lies so close to London that, had it not been for post-war planning restrictions, it would have been swamped by housing.

The proximity of the metropolis is felt in several ways. Firstly, there is the large amount of land used solely for public recreation that is encountered in Surrey – Box Hill and Albury Downs for example. The sheer weight of numbers using such areas can leave visible wear on the land.

Greenbelt designation also aims to protect farmland from despoliation and development. Certainly farmland has been protected in Surrey, and we can see the green fields and fine old hedgerow trees rolling to the doorsteps of the suburbs. But this can be misleading. Farmland close to cities is rarely farmed as it is in the deeper countryside.

One of the reasons that such a picturesque and traditional landscape remains over much of Surrey is that the land is under-used. This is because farms tend to be small or broken up into smaller pieces by roads, housing and so on and are thus less amenable to intensive use. They may be disturbed by the public or even under the ownership of people who do not farm. So to some extent the land is 'fossilized' and has escaped many of the more extreme post-war changes in the countryside. There are other factors at work, of course, but the difference between the intensively farmed sweeps of much of the Kent Downs and the tight patchwork of woods and small fields seen between Reigate and Dorking is at least partly a result of the relation between farming efficiency and the nearness of the capital.

It is no coincidence that the North Downs and the Greensand hills nearby have many working and disused quarries. The resources are there, otherwise the quarries would not be, but the materials extracted – chalk, sandstone, sands and gravels – are by no means rare elsewhere in Britain. But the nearness of London means that they have been obtained from those areas closest to the demand to cut down transport costs. Surrey sandstone is in many a London building.

The pressure of the ever-expanding city always makes itself felt. London is constricted by its greenbelt, so it has burst out along transport corridors or to affect the growth of towns all over the South East. It also makes itself felt by road schemes like the M25, which cuts through the greenbelt to bypass the congested sprawl, or the improved major roads radiating out from it. At Merstham can be seen all the bad impacts of being situated on the edge of a city. There is the massive motorway intersection of the M25 and M23, the sprawl of housing estates and areas of farmland hemmed in by roads and houses and, as a result, neglected. This is the 'urban fringe' at its visual worst.

At its best, it encompasses the majority of the Surrey rural landscape. The beauty of the countryside around Box Hill and Ranmore Common is in complete contrast to Merstham. The Surrey greenbelt is, in general, a visual success. London has been kept at bay in this area, and some superb English landscape has been saved.

It is probably best to leave Westerham by the A233, although, it is tedious to begin a day's walk beside a main road. However, proceed beyond the edge of Westerham for almost a mile as far as the second turning on the left – a private road, called 'The Avenue', marked by a North Downs Way plinth. Go down here for about a mile until meeting a road, with a postbox opposite the junction. Turn right here, now leaving the North Downs Way, and then go first left over a stile. The path runs along the edge of a wood and a line of trees before bearing to the right and entering a second field.

In the second field go left along a hedgerow and follow it to a road. Turn left at the road, and then go over the first stile on the right that you come to. Proceed beside the left-hand hedge as far as a stile on the left. Cross it and head in a diagonal across the next field to the B2024.

Cross over the road and over the stile on its far side. There is a good viewpoint here of the very thickly wooded Greensand hills with Westerham down to the left and Oxted down on the right.

Follow the path beside the hedgerow on the right. Go across the middle of the next field on a clear path towards the trees. There is a stile where the path meets the woods, and it forks after crossing this stile. Take the right-hand fork.

When you meet a road, go straight over and up the stepped path opposite.

Follow the waymarked path ahead, crossing two stiles *en route*. This route comes down beside and slightly above the B269 for some way before ending at a junction of the B269 and B2024. Walk over the junction towards a house ahead and then turn left down a track just before reaching the house. There is a North Downs Way signpost here. Go down the track through woodland and take the first path on the right that you come to. This path contours around the scarp slope through beech woods for almost a mile.

On the far side of the woodland there is a junction of paths. The route now turns downhill on a well-defined section with a rope handrail and yellow arrows to point the way. Follow this path all the way to a stile at the bottom of the hill, ignoring any minor paths off to either side on the way down. Once over this stile, turn right and walk along the hedgerow for 50 yards to the next stile, then go across a field around the slope on a clear path as far as a stile. Cross this and turn left. You are now on the North Downs Way again, and should follow the fence down to a road.

Turn right at the road, walk for 50 yards and then turn left onto a path. Take this path across the field towards an area of trees extending out from the foot of the scarp. Go on past the trees as far as a signpost standing prominently in the middle of the field, where you turn right and follow a clear path up onto the scarp slope as far as another signpost. Turn left here and walk along the slope into an area of scrub. Shortly after entering the scrub, the path turns right clearly uphill via a long series of steps. These take you up on to South Hawke, and at the top of the steps there is another signpost which directs to the left. Following this course means that you eventually strike the road on the hilltop. When you do so, keep straight on to the road junction on Tandridge Hill. Take the left fork here. The road can be followed by way of a footpath set slightly above it on the right. The path eventually arrives at a stile, crosses it and bears away to the right uphill.

When you meet a road, go straight across and into the woods ahead. Turn left at the next path junction. Continue on, ignoring a path coming in from the left, and then descend into a dry valley where there is a track running beside a house. Go left past the house (South Lodge). Keep on as far as the next signpost, where you should turn left and will then meet a minor road shortly afterwards. Cross over the road onto a path opposite. Follow the path as far as a track, where you should turn right.

Turn left at the next signpost, cross a stile and proceed over a road-bridge above the A22. Having crossed the bridge, continue ahead up the road on the other side. Take the first path off the road on the left. It is marked by a plinth. Walk into the woods and keep on the clearest path ahead, ignoring any other paths that join.

Go left when you meet a road. There is an excellent viewpoint here as far as the South Downs, with Chanctonbury Ring prominently in view. Turn left onto a bridleway at the far end of the open viewpoint. When the bridleway forks, bear right. At the next fork you should bear left. Having travelled around the side of Gravelly Hill in this way, you will eventually come out at a road. Go left here (not down Hextalls Lane) and walk for over half a mile to a road junction. Turn right, then immediately left at the junction onto a farm road.

Once on the farm road, take the right fork and proceed on ahead. Views now open up to the south-west over Redhill and Reigate, with Reigate Hill and the North Downs scarp stretching away beyond. Turn right at the next farm road junction, and from here stay on the main route ahead for roughly three-quarters of a mile. Cross over the road and carry on along the track on the other side. Notice the Fullers Earth works over on the Greensand ridge at this point, just east of Redhill. When the track meets a field, bear left and strike across the field to the left of, and below, a copse.

Note: This is probably the ugliest place that the whole walk ever meets between Dover and Beachy Head, but unfortunately in order to travel the North Downs it has to be negotiated.

Beside the copse the path continues down to a gate, now clearly in view in the hedge at the bottom of the field.

Go through the gate and into the next field beyond. Then bear right across the field – the path is just visible.

Walk down to a point beside the motorway and go under it by way of the subway(!). Having gone through the subway, turn left and follow the clear waymarking around the edge of the field to a road. Turn right at the road and walk along it all the way to the A23. Go across the A23 and down Gatton Bottom on the other side.

Turn left opposite the church and use the footbridge to cross the motorway to Merstham. When you come out at Quality Street in Merstham, turn left, and then turn right as indicated by the North Downs Way signpost. Walk down this path, crossing two stiles by the cricket pitch, and continue straight ahead to a third stile. The path is faint, but just visible.

After crossing the third stile, go up across the field to the skyline. Again, the path is difficult to discern. Once on the crest of the hill, head towards the nearest end of a line of trees over on the left when they come into view, as they will, on the hilltop. Once you have reached the trees, walk beside them to their right. The path crosses a stile, goes through a gate and then merges with a track.

Where the track meets a road, turn right and then left through a set of white gates down a private road – it is marked by a North Downs Way signpost, so should not be confused with a track going off to the left just before it. Walk on through the school buildings, using the clear North Downs waymarks for guidance. Once past the buildings, carry straight on until you almost meet the minor road running beside the motorway. Just before meeting the road, turn left up a bridleway. From here on the path tends to contain a number of forks and confusing sections, but they all seem to end up on the top of Quarry

Hill. From the top of the hill there is an excellent view across Reigate and the Surrey Weald.

To get down into Reigate, it is best to walk down beside the A217 along the pavement. The minor road running down the side of Quarry Hill to Wray Common is very dangerous for pedestrians lower down and is to be avoided.

Reigate
Accommodation: This is plentiful in Reigate and the surrounding area.
Public transport: Reigate is well provided, being highly accessible from many areas by train. There are also bus services. It is possible to return to Westerham by bus.
Parking: This is plentiful.

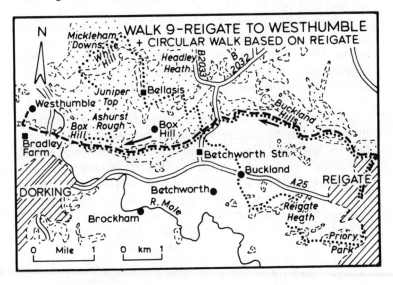

9th Walk: Reigate to Westhumble
Total distance: 8 miles
OS map: 187 Dorking, Reigate and Crawley

Stage 1: Reigate to Box Hill

Leave Reigate by walking beside the A217 up Reigate Hill. The landmark to look for is the Yew Tree pub, which is on the left part way up the hill. Walk about 150 yards past the Yew Tree and take the first bridleway on the left. Just after joining the bridleway it forks, and you should take the left-hand (unmade) fork which runs behind some gardens.

Note: The next section of the walk (between the asterisks in the text) takes you up onto Reigate Hill and Colley Hill with excellent views to be enjoyed there. However, it does include a very steep and tricky descent on a slippery slope. You may prefer to keep on ahead, bearing slightly left, at the estate road to follow the foot of the scarp instead. Route-finding is easy and rejoins the text at the second asterisk.

* On meeting a small estate road, go straight across, bearing right up the path opposite between two white posts. The climb up onto the crest of the Downs now begins, and with it comes the view. Once on the hilltop, simply follow the crest of the scarp around towards Colley Hill.

After passing a stand of pine trees on the scarp slope to the left, the path passes through a hedgerow by way of a narrow gap, and then continues on the other side along Colley Hill – defined by an area of shortened sward. When the path comes up against woodland, it continues straight into the trees and then drops down the scarp slope through the woodland. The worn areas are clear enough to follow here, but it really is a very dangerous route and atrocious in the wet on the slippery downhill walk.

Towards the bottom of the hill you meet a deeply eroded path, where you turn left and continue downhill. This then comes out onto the North Downs Way at the foot of the scarp, where there are horse-barriers to the left and right. Turn right here.*

The walking is now simple along the foot of Juniper Hill

and the Buckland Hills. The path is enclosed by bushes in places and open in others, and there are occasional wayfinding posts to avoid problems at path junctions.

Proceed in this manner for well over a mile, having, by this stage, passed a path on the left and on the right. Having travelled this distance, you come to a broader path. Go right here and begin to ascend. After passing a small disused quarry (off the path on the right), look for an indistinct path going down to the left. It is visible only as a slightly worn area at first, but after a few yards becomes clear and easy to follow.

Note: If you do go past this path, there is a much clearer path on the left further on which meets the first one near the foot of the scarp; so this can be used instead.

On meeting another path, turn left. The route now leaves the woods on the scarp and heads across a field towards the end of a line of trees. Once arrived at the line of trees, there is a stile and signpost. Cross the stile and walk along the avenue of trees to the B2032. Turn left along the road. The pavement along the left-hand side of the road ends just before a bend. At this point cross over to the right-hand side of the road and follow the signposted path just to one side of it. The path comes down to a pavement. Keep going through Betchworth and take the first turning on the right. (If you go as far as Betchworth Station, you have missed it by a long way.)

Walk up the road and then take the first junction on the left, an unmade road. Where this road forks, take a right. After passing some houses, the track narrows to a path and passes Betchworth Quarries. Stick to the main path, avoiding any that come in from either side. On meeting the large quarry floor, turn left onto a track. Follow the track round between old brick arches, after which it becomes a path again. As the path climbs up around the hillside towards the top of the Downs, there are wide-ranging views again before entering into woodland.

Follow the path up into the trees and then take a left

turn by a waymarking post up a set of steps cut in a bank. Keep on around the lip of the scarp above Brockham Warren and turn left at the next path junction. Now the path begins to descend again. Watch for a gap in the trees on the way down with a view back to Reigate Hill.

Part-way down the hill there are waymarking posts. Turn right here and up a set of steps. The next junction is with a track on a bend, where you should fork right. This is now a broad, stony path. Where the way is barred by a gate, turn left and walk downhill. Then follow a fence around to the right and along the path contouring along the slope. Go straight across the next path met. From here it becomes unclear, but there are waymarking posts to mark the way. Follow these out onto the open area of Box Hill, one of the most well-known viewpoints in the South East.

Stage 2: Box Hill to Westhumble

Go to the triangulation pillar and continue on past on a clear path. Straight ahead, on the other side of the Mole valley, the spire of Ranmore church should be in view ahead.

Once back into woodland, follow the waymarked path down the hill. It is stepped and boarded in a number of places. Turn right at the next junction and follow the waymarking posts through the trees and down to the River Mole – which can be crossed by stepping-stones.

Walk straight ahead on the other side of the river as far as the A24. From here turn left and walk beside the road for about 75 yards. Then cross to the far side and walk down a minor road with a North Downs Way signpost pointing down it. This road is metalled, though very narrow, and runs through a strip of woodland between fields.

At the first junction of paths (about half a mile down the minor road), it is possible to go either left into Dorking (via Bradley Farm) or right into Westhumble. From

Westhumble you can use public transport to get to Dorking.

Circular walk based on Reigate
Total distance: 17 miles
OS map: 187 Dorking, Reigate and Crawley
For the outward section of this walk read Stage 1 of the Reigate to Westhumble route.

Stage 2: Box Hill, via White Hill, to the Box Hill/Pebble Common road
Note: You can greatly shorten this walk by excluding the tour out over Juniper Top, White Hill and Headley Heath. If you wish to do this, walk along the road eastwards from Box Hill past Box Hill village and read from Stage 3 onwards.

It is necessary to retrace steps from the triangulation pillar for a short distance. Walk up to the road that runs along Box Hill above the viewpoint. Turn right at the road and walk along beside it for about half a mile. You will have travelled the distance once past two lay-bys, then a driveway bordered by rustic fencing and finally a large parking-area. All of these are on the left-hand side of the road. When past the large parking-area, take the second path on the left, which is very clearly visible. (If you go as far as the village of Box Hill, you have missed the path. The path we want is immediately before the first building of the village.)

Stay on the largest path. It is not easy because there are masses of other marked and unmarked paths in this woodland. If in doubt, use a compass to maintain a check on direction, bearing in mind that the short-term objective is Juniper Top.

The path eventually enters a clearing on Juniper Top and then comes out onto open downland, where you should follow the broad swathe of short sward down the hill. Juniper Hall is visible in the dry valley below.

Follow the path down to the valley bottom where it meets a track. Turn right here and take the track as far as a road. Cross the road and walk straight ahead up the steep path opposite. This is a very steep climb on earth and rock and needs great care in wet conditions. Near the top of the hill the path makes a right turn and then contours around the hillside.

When the path forks, there are two alternatives:

1. Take the right fork and head around the side of White Hill until the path again meets the road. This is a shorter distance, and it is easier to find the way. It comes out at the road at the same point as the longer alternative.

2. Fork left (uphill). Take care to stay on the path. At first it is possible to follow a line of old iron fenceposts around to the left. Where the fence ends, turn right. The path here is very unclear. It may be safer to take a compass bearing to the clearing on the top of White Hill, which is the short-term target.

   At the next, rather indistinct, junction, bear left and you will soon meet a clear, broad path. Turn right, and it comes out to the open area on White Hill. Turn right here and follow the edge of woods all the way to the furthest end of the clearing. Once there, you meet another path. Turn right here on a very clear path, then turn first right fifty yards downhill beside the nature reserve. Now go down the steep slope to the foot of the hill. At the hill bottom you meet the road in the dry valley – this is where alternative routes 1 and 2 meet up again. If, at the foot of the hill, you come to a path, you need to walk left along it for a short distance in order to come to the road.

Turn left, then immediately right at the road and take the path up the other side of the dry valley. Towards the top of the hill there is a path junction by a National Trust sign. Go straight on here, and in less than 50 yards you meet a small private road. Turn left and walk along the road.

Follow the road as far as the edge of Box Hill village, and then go left onto a gated bridleway, situated just before a fork in the road. In front of the gate there is a wide car-parking area.

Stay on this track, ignoring any paths off to either side. It drops down into a hollow and then climbs out again. Once out of the hollow, follow the stony path around to the right at a junction with a ride.

Note: There are plenty of confusing paths along this section of Headley Heath, but hopefully the instructions are clear enough to avoid problems.

Keep on the path in the same general direction, and eventually you will be walking beside a wire fence. Follow the fence until it turns sharply away from the path, at which point carry on ahead and leave it.

When you meet a broad track running by a lone house, go right and follow the track all the way to a road. Turn left at the road and walk along it for about a quarter of a mile.

Stage 3: Box Hill/Pebble Common road to Reigate
Now look for a signposted footpath on the right. It is easily missed. If you walk down the road as far as 'Dukes Wood', you would have missed the footpath by about 150 yards.

The path is easy to follow at first, but take care when it comes to an area of very large, old beech trees. The path is invisible here and leaves the area over to the left-hand side. Walk as far as a large cedar tree standing beside the path within the woodland and turn right, downhill, even though the path ahead may appear clearer. Now follow this path all the way down towards Betchworth Station. When you meet a drive, turn right and then follow a private road to the B2032, where you should go left.

Take the first minor road on the right to leave the B2032. Once on this minor road, turn right to Holmes

Farm. Before you reach the house at Holmes Farm, turn left onto a footpath. The path runs between fences and then heads out across a field beside a wooden fence to a stile. Cross the stile and follow the railway cutting down to track level. Cross the railway tracks and go straight across the field on the other side. In the second field, walk parallel to the left-hand hedge towards a house. There is a gate to the right of the house. Go through the gate and follow the path to a road. Turn right at the road and walk all the way into Buckland and the A25.

Cross the A25 and go down the road opposite in front of the post office and shop. Once past these buildings, go left down Dungates Lane. Where the lane divides, go left and follow the bridlepath sign. The bridlepath goes past a massive sand and gravel pit, and Reigate Heath windmill comes into view ahead with views of the North Downs over to the left. Continue down this way as far as Dungates Farm. Beyond the farm it becomes a track; stay on it as far as a signpost directing you left on a footpath. On meeting a stile, go left along the field boundary, following a clear line of waymarking stakes. You then have to cross another stile and continue to follow the left-hand hedge in the next field.

Note: The footpath shown on the map has been re-routed to go the other side of the windmill to that drawn. For this reason the map will not agree with conditions 'on the ground'. Keep to these directions to avoid problems.

Keep walking until level with a large gap in the left-hand hedgerow with a gateway and fencing in. At this point turn right, at right angles to the hedge, and go across this corner of the field to the hedge on the other side. Once there, follow the hedge ahead to a stile. Cross the stile and follow the path as far as a track near the A25. Go straight over the track and cut across the 'rough land' on the edge of Reigate Heath until you meet a broad, grassy ride. On meeting the ride, turn right and follow it all the way to a road.

Turn right at the road and walk down it as far as a turning on the left, called Bonny's Road.

Walk down Bonny's Road until it forks. Take the right fork, then go left after less than 50 yards onto a path. Now keep on this path, deeply cut for the most part, until you meet a minor road. Turn left at the road and follow it to a junction. Go straight ahead at the junction onto the path opposite, clearly shown by a flight of steps. At the top of the steps there are three paths to choose from. Take the middle one, ahead up the hill. There are good views from the hilltop triangulation pillar across Reigate and the Surrey countryside all around. Beyond the triangulation pillar follow the path ahead into the trees. On meeting another path, which becomes tarmacked further down the hill, go left. This now takes you down into Reigate.

10th Walk: Westhumble to Artington

Total distance: 14 miles
OS maps: 187 Dorking, Reigate and Crawley; 186 Aldershot and Guildford

Westhumble/Dorking

Although Westhumble is the actual 'staging post' of the walks, it is in easy public transport, and even walking, distance of Dorking. Also, as Dorking has the facilities lacking at Westhumble, it is best to think of them as a pair.

Accommodation: Plentiful in Dorking.

Public transport: Highly accessible. Three railway stations in Dorking and bus services. Possible to return to Reigate from Dorking or from Artington to Dorking if needed.

Parking: Plentiful in Dorking. Non-existent in West-humble.

Stage 1: Westhumble to Oaken Grove

These directions read from Westhumble Station. However,

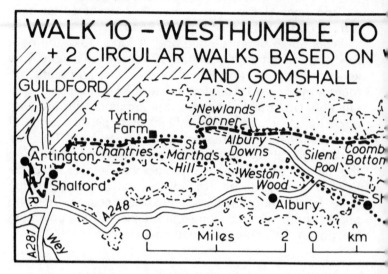

WALK 10 – WESTHUMBLE TO
+ 2 CIRCULAR WALKS BASED ON
AND GOMSHALL

GUILDFORD

Tyting Farm

Newlands Corner

Artington

Chantries

St Martha's Hill

Albury Downs

Silent Pool

Coomb Botton

Shalford

Weston Wood

Albury

A248

R. Wey

A281

0   Miles   2   0   km

in a short distance they meet the path junction between Bradley Farm and Westhumble (the finishing-point of the Reigate – Westhumble walk), so you may prefer to come in at that point if starting at Dorking rather than Westhumble – the asterisk denotes this point. (Remember to go left instead of right at the first instruction, as you will be coming from the other direction.)

From Westhumble Station, go up the road through the village until past the white fenced entrance to Pilgrims' Way. Fifty yards past here is a path on the left. It is a very narrow entrance and needs to be looked for carefully. The path then runs between gardens and meets a field. Go straight across the field to a belt of woodland ahead. Running down the centre of the belt of woodland is a minor surfaced track. You are now at the path junction between Bradley Farm and Westhumble, previously referred to.

* Turn right here and follow the track on its slightly uphill course as far as the first junction, where you go left and then straight on uphill past a left-hand turning (about 50 yards on from the first junction).

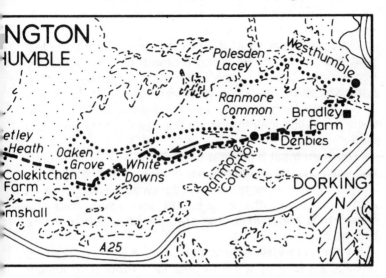

A little further on there is a crossroads of tracks. Go straight on here. Eventually the trees are left behind to give extensive views. Follow this path around the side of the hill, climbing most of the way, until the path is blocked by a gate at the grounds of 'Denbies'. Go right here and follow the line of the fence. When you meet a road, go left and walk along the broad roadside verge until past Ranmore Church. Walk on as far as a road junction. Go right at the junction and then immediately left down a signposted footpath. Cross the stile here and walk on until over a second stile. Just past the second stile, fork right and follow the hedgerow. There are views over to Westcott and Leith Hill. Where the hedgerow bends sharply around to the right, continue on straight ahead across the field to a gateway and walk on into the woodland.

The next section of the route involves keeping to the main path at the numerous junctions coming in from either side. First there are paths coming in from the left and right, and a second from the left a little further on. After this a bridlepath is crossed. Where the path encounters a bridleway, there are offset horse-barriers to keep riders off the footpath.

Go straight across at the next bridlepath junction. Just past this junction, the broad footpath you are following bends right. Leave it here and walk straight ahead on a narrower path. There is a waymarking post at this point. The narrow path can be rather indistinct in places, but there are yellow paintmarks on the trees to help show the way.

You then meet a broader path. Turn left here, downhill, and walk on past an old pillbox.

You then emerge from the woods with views eastwards along the escarpment and south over the Surrey Hills and Weald. You are now on a part of White Downs.

At the next waymarking post, turn right and head up through an area of scrub to another narrow path, where you should turn left and walk on past several pillboxes as far as a road. Turn left and walk down the road until you come to a pillbox on the right. Go right here, up a path running beside the pillbox. This is a steep climb. Ignore a path on the left part-way up the hill, but just past it fork left. You now pass through some woodland before coming out onto open downland. On meeting a path, turn right, ignoring a path on the right just after having turned, and keep on through the woods as far as a broad track.

Stage 2: Oaken Grove to Netley Heath

Turn left at the track and follow it along, ignoring paths off to either side. Eventually the track becomes a small metalled road. Keep on until you reach the area known as Netley Heath on the map — though it is essentially woodland here. At this point the path comes up from Colekitchen Farm to meet the road.

Stage 3: Netley Heath to Shalford/Artington

Stay on the metalled road, ignoring those roads which join

with it on Netley Heath. Now walk along the road all the way to a set of stables – a distance of about one mile. After passing the stables, there is a junction of tracks; bear right here and then go first left afterwards.

On meeting a road, turn right and walk as far as a road junction, where you should go left. Now take the first bridlepath on the left. Keep on this path for about 1¾ miles all the way to the A25 at Albury Downs. Take care not to divert off at any of the path junctions *en route*.

Go straight across the A25 and walk ahead across the viewpoint car-park until over at its far end. Continue on here along a clear bridlepath as far as the first path crossroads. Turn left here and walk as far as a road. Go left here. There is a footpath running along the right-hand side of the road most of the distance, so you can avoid traffic much of the time.

Walk as far as two bridlepaths coming in at a corner of the road.

Here there are two choices, depending on whether you are doing the round-trip walk from Gomshall or are only going one way between Westhumble and Shalford.

1. If going one way only, it is best to go up onto St Martha's Hill at this point to take in the view, meeting up with the alternative route at GR 016484.

2 If undertaking the circular walk, St Martha's Hill is perhaps best saved until the return trip. Therefore take the first bridlepath (going off right rather than straight ahead) and walk along between the fields at the foot of the hills. Go straight across the road near Tyting Farm. Stay on the main path. Pass a path coming in from the left. At the second junction of paths you are at GR 016484 where the alternative route from St Martha's Hill comes down.

Continue straight on until the third junction of paths encountered, where you should go right. (This is in fact a crossroads, though only three paths are mapped.) Now keep on along the main path past South Warren Farm and all the way to a cottage beside the track (Chantry Cottage) on the edge of a 'green'. Take the first path left beside this cottage and follow it as far as a road on the outskirts of Shalford.

Here you can choose either to go into Shalford and on to Artington to end the one-way walk from Westhumble or to begin the return leg of the circular walk. (For this last option see Stage 3 of the circular walk based on Gomshall).

Stage 4: Shalford to Artington

At the estate road take the path running ahead beside the left side of the road and follow it as far as a lane. Go straight across this road and take the signposted footpath on the far side across the fields and past a converted mill to the A281. Go right at the road and then first left down a signposted bridleway. Now keep on until coming to a junction with a path on the right. There is a stile here. Go over the stile and cross the field to the river bank. Follow the River Wey along to the left as far as a footbridge at a weir pool. Cross the bridge and follow the bank around all the way to the lock gates on the canalized section of river. Go over the footbridge at the lock gates and then keep on towards the railway arch and beyond to the A3100 at Artington.

Artington

Artington has little to offer as a walker's rest. However, this is unimportant because of its proximity to Guildford, from where you can return to Artington the next day.

Accommodation: Available in Guildford.

Public transport: Trains from Shalford (next door to Artington) into Guildford or back to Dorking. Buses into Guildford.

Parking: Best to park in Guildford and take a bus out to Artington.

Circular walk based on Westhumble
Total distance: 10 miles
OS map: 187 Dorking, Reigate and Crawley
The furthest extent of this walk is Oaken Grove, on the
Downs to the north-east of Gomshall. For the outward leg
of this walk, read Stage 1 of the Westhumble to Artington
route.

Stage 2: Oaken Grove to Westhumble
Turn right at the broad track. If it is wet and badly rutted,
there is a drier path just to one side of it after several
hundred yards. Now keep straight on through the
woodland until you come to a path junction on the edge of
the trees where they meet fields. Go right here and stay
on the main path to a road. Cross the road and walk ahead
as far as another road, where you should go right. Now
follow the road onto Ranmore Common. After some
distance it is possible to walk on a footpath beside the
road. Maintain this direction for about a mile. There are
numerous paths off to the left, most of them bridlepaths.
The one to take is that which goes left at GR 134504.
This is signposted with a direction arm (do not take the
other path going off at this point which is marked only by
a post).
Note: Many of the paths and tracks on Ranmore
Common do not appear on the map. If in doubt, follow
these directions – unless you're already lost, in which case
they'll be fairly useless!

Follow the path to a clearing in the woodland and keep
straight on at the junction here. After this the path meets
some tracks. Cross one track and then walk along the
main one beyond for about 100 yards and go right on a
path. Go 200 yards down this path and then turn first
right. Turn left at the next path junction and keep going
until you meet a track, where you should go right. Stay on
the track until it leaves the woods, and then take the next
path on the right which leads clearly across a field. There

are the remains of a stile by the gate at the junction which shows the meeting of the paths.

On the far side of the field there is another path. Turn left and walk past Bagden Farm to a road. Go right at the road and then right at the first road junction you come to. Walk past a group of houses on the left, and then take the path through the first field gateway on the left past them. The path is unsignposted and indistinct, so follow the hedgerow. Look over to the right from here, and Ranmore spire is in view.

On the far side of the field the path meets woodland. Skirt the lower edge of the woods. There is a clear path with a fence on the left. On the far side of the woodland there is a stile. Cross it and proceed straight ahead along a fence. Box Hill is in prominent view ahead.

On meeting a line of telegraph poles, follow them over to the right to the far hedge where there is a stile. Go over it onto a path the other side. Turn left and take the path to a track. Go left along the track and follow it as far as a path on the right with a gate across its entrance. Go down this. On meeting a road, go right to get into Westhumble.

Circular walk based on Gomshall
Total distance: 13 miles
OS maps: 187 Dorking, Reigate and Crawley; 186 Aldershot and Guildford.

Gomshall
Accommodation: Sparse, to say the least! However, as Gomshall is so easily accessible from Dorking or Guildford, this is not a problem.
Public transport: Trains to Dorking and Guildford. Buses also provide links with these towns.
Parking: Difficult. You will probably have to resort to a kerbside. Failing that, it might be best to park in Dorking and come out by public transport.

Stage 1: Gomshall to Netley Heath

Leave Gomshall by a No Through Road (that turns off the A25 opposite Gomshall Tanneries Ltd), called Colekitchen Lane. It is approximately a third of a mile on the Guildford side of Gomshall railway station.

Now follow it all the way to Colekitchen Farm, passing any path junctions on the way. The road is unmade on the final length to the farm. The track narrows to a path at Colekitchen Farm. Follow the path all the way up to a metalled road on Netley Heath.

Stage 2: Netley Heath to Shalford

See Stage 3 of the Westhumble to Artington walk.

Stage 3: Shalford to Gomshall

When you meet the estate road on the outskirts of Shalford, turn almost immediately left onto a signposted footpath across a field. Continue along on a very clear line, following the course of an old hedgerow that you meet part-way through the field. Turn left when you come to a farm track and walk along it until 50 yards beyond a signposted footpath on the right. Here there is an unsignposted footpath on the left, marked only by a rather overgrown stile. Cross this and the path behind climbs up onto a steep-sided hill offering a good viewpoint.

You are now on a 'ridge'. Continue east on the path of short sward towards St Martha's Hill, which is clearly visible ahead as a wooded hill with a church on top. When you see a stile on the left, go over it and you meet a clear path along the edge of the woods, where you should turn right and follow the path. The path broadens to a track and then meets a road.

Turn left at the road and then turn first right onto a worn path to the top of St Martha's Hill.

Go past the church and down the hillside on a very clear path. Walk down to the car-park at the foot of the

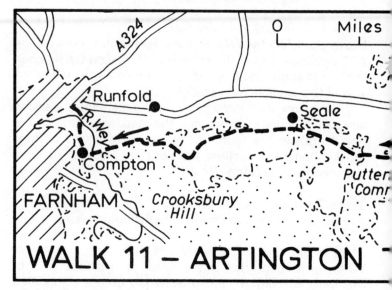

hill, situated beside a road. Turn right at the road, and then go first left down a signposted path which is clear to follow. At the next junction of paths, turn right and walk for 100 yards before turning left onto a path that follows a fence across a field. (The map misleadingly shows this as a straightforward crossroads junction – but the paths are in fact offset.)

Keep following the fence and it leads to a gate. Go through the gate, and the path then runs between fences. On meeting a track, go left, then immediately right. At the next junction go straight on over a stile.

Go straight over the quarry road when you meet it and continue ahead through the trees to a field, which is to be crossed beside the left-hand boundary. Cross over the A248 and continue ahead on the path opposite. After 200 yards there is a stile. Cross this and go ahead across the field beyond – though the path is indistinct. On the far side of the field, cross a stile beside a gate and follow the path ahead across an area of rough woodland, avoiding any

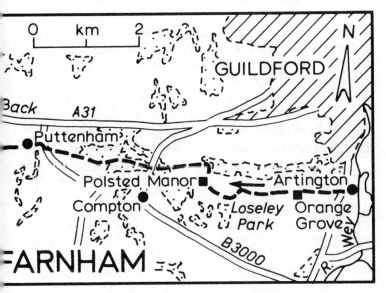

paths off to either side. Continue straight ahead over the field on the far side of the woodland as far as a road.

Turn right at the road and walk along it until you have crossed the Tilling Bourne. Then go left across a field, following the stream. Turn left on meeting a track and follow it to a road. Go right at the road and into Shere. Go straight across at the main crossroads in Shere and walk until level with the church. Here go right on a signposted footpath opposite the church.

Turn left at the next signposted path junction. The path eventually broadens to a track and then meets a road on the edge of Gomshall. Turn left at the road to get into the village.

11th Walk: Artington to Farnham
Total distance: 11 miles
OS map; 186 Aldershot and Guildford.
Return to the point in Artington at which the previous

day's walk ended. From here walk a little further down the A3100 in a southerly direction and take the first road on the right, where there is also a footpath signpost.

Follow the road until it turns sharp right, where you should go on straight ahead up a green lane. This then goes clearly between the fields, becoming metalled at the first of the houses on the edge of Littleton. Continue on to the road in Littleton, where you should go straight on to the path opposite. Again, the path is very clear as it crosses the first field. However, in the next field the path is indistinct, so aim ahead past a large oak tree and then, on drawing level with it, the stile on the far side of the field comes into clear view.

Go over the stile and on past a small lake. Keep on ahead beside a left-hand fence. About 50 yards after crossing a track, follow the fence where it turns sharply left. After a further 50 yards there is a stile on the left. Cross this and continue to maintain the same direction beside the fence. Go over the next stile and turn right at the track beyond. Walk as far as the junction at Polsted Manor. Turn right here and walk up a deeply cut path. Follow it all the way to a signposted junction with the North Downs Way, where you should go left.

Turn left on meeting a road, and then go first right onto another path. Follow it under a road bridge and then bear left where the track forks. The route then enters an area of woodland. When you come to a fork, bear right. Go straight on at the next path junction. The path then joins a track where you turn right and go past Puttenham Heath golf course. Where the track eventually meets a road, continue straight ahead all the way to the B3000.

Turn right here and then go first left down the road to Puttenham.

Walk all the way through Puttenham to its furthest end, where there is a No Through Road, called Lascombe Lane, on a right-hand bend in the road. Go down Lascombe Lane as far as a junction with another minor road. Go right here and follow this minor road until it ends. Once it ends, continue ahead on a path that gradually climbs up onto Puttenham Common.

At the top of the hill there is a path junction, where you should bear right. After about 150 yards there is another junction. Go right here.

Eventually the path drops downhill on the other side of the common to a path junction waymarked by a post, where you turn right. Next you meet a track. Turn right here and after 100 yards the track meets a road. Turn left at the road and then go first right immediately past a house on the right-hand side of the road. Now go up through woodland, over a stile and into a field beyond. Follow the wire fence ahead through the field until you are to the far side of a block of pine trees (Note: these trees are to the left of the fence; the path passes them but does not go through them), where you should go left over two stiles into another field. On the other side of the field the path enters woodland for 50 yards before turning right and going through the trees to a clearing. The route may become confusing at the clearing as it is ill defined. Bear right through it and look for a waymarking post to confirm the way.

On meeting a road, turn right and then take the first path on the left. Now go straight ahead on a clear path across the fields, crossing a track *en route*. At the far side of the large field, turn right to cross a stile, then go left on its other side. Walk along beside the pine trees to the next stile. Cross this and turn left on the path beyond. Go straight over a road when you meet it. The path now runs beside a golf course and then meets another road. Turn left and follow the road all the way to a road junction, where you go right and walk along the road until within sight of the next junction. In this area look for a signposted path on the left which 'cuts the corner' between the roads. When the short path meets a road, turn left and walk for less than 50 yards before going right on a path into an area of woodland.

Carry on as far as the next signpost, where you should go right. Just before reaching the edge of the woodland, turn left up a set of steps and cross a stile. Then, at the edge of the woods, cross another stile and proceed on a clear path line through fields (meeting a small patch of woodland *en route*). The course of the path is clearly shown by a series of stiles and signposts.

On meeting a road, turn right and walk downhill to Moor Park School beside the River Wey. To get into Farnham from here, cross the river and turn right at the road junction beyond. Now take the first footpath on the right. Turn left at the next path junction you come to and then right at the one beyond. Follow this path under the railway and into the centre of Farnham.

Farnham
Accommodation: This is plentiful in Farnham.
Public transport: There is a railway station and bus services. It is possible to return to Guildford from Farnham if desired.
Parking: Plentiful.

7

The Story of the
South East Woodlands

When walking along the raised backs of the Downs, there are wide views across the Weald as an almost constant companion. The woodland is in places so extensive and the high timbered hedgerows so tall that often, when we look out across it, the illusion is of a vast, continuous forest. It serves to give an impression of its natural appearance, much as it must have looked to our distant ancestors. But it is just an impression, for the Wealden landscape today is wholly artificial and is the result of centuries of human activity.

Perhaps the hardest thing to establish is when the natural woodland first began to be altered. As more information emerges, it becomes apparent that Britain was fairly extensively cleared of its forest cover much earlier than was previously thought, quite possibly during the New Stone Age. However, large tracts of forest remained, and it would seem likely that the Weald was one of these, when the unsuitability of the heavy soils for the purposes of early agriculture is considered. Also, accounts indicate a large Wealden forest as late as Saxon times.

It was the Saxon period, then, that saw the beginning of large-scale changes in the Weald forest. Clearances were being made at this time in some areas, and place-names hold clues to where this occurred. The place-name components to look for are 'ley', 'den', 'hurst', 'wold', 'field', 'leigh' and 'stock'.

Look at a map including any area of the Weald and you will see these name components liberally sprinkled right into the heart of the former forest. This suggests that a considerable amount of colonization took place prior to the Norman Conquest.

Another thing to look for is an example of where a village developed around the original forest clearing, giving perhaps a very large green.

It is also striking on a map showing the Weald how, in many areas, the roads appear to have been 'raked' across the landscape in roughly parallel lines. This is particularly apparent, for example, in the area east of Ditchling (OS Sheet 198 Brighton and The Downs) where the roads clearly run northwards from the foot of the scarp. This is a Saxon pattern and developed because of the unique natural conditions of the region. What happened is that the 'islands' of colonized land in the Weald belonged to landowners located on the already farmed superior soils of the Downs or Downs foot. In order to reach the newly won outposts in the forest, it was necessary to drive stock across intervening land, and as a result a pattern of roughly parallel roads developed, linking the areas together.

A great many are now metalled and functional; many are quiet green lanes or used just as farm tracks. Several of these routes are briefly used on the walks.

As the Weald was cleared outwards from the foot of the Downs and around the forest clearings, the newly won land had to be divided up. It is uncertain if the Saxons did in fact split land up into small parcels. They may well have farmed in broad, open fields. Much land at the foot of the Downs seems never to have been hedged – for example, the Adur basin north of Steyning and Upper Beeding presents a very open landscape, as does the area around Wye in Kent.

Nevertheless it is a common characteristic of the Weald – and, indeed, of parts of the Downs – to see field boundaries comprising thick belts of woodland. These are called 'shaws', and whilst some are Saxon, most are probably much later in origin. It also needs to be remembered that much of the forest, though not cleared, would have been managed in various ways for timber products and thus altered, from the natural state.

By the time of the Norman Conquest, then, the South East was a fairly well-developed region although there were still many areas of remote, untouched woodland. The final extensive clearances went ahead in the two centuries following the Conquest. In medieval times fields were cleared from the forest ('assarting'), and although the landscape seldom shows when a particular area was opened up, place-names including 'ridden', 'stocking' and 'close' can point to this period.

This was also the time when the majority of shaws were created. Shaws were made by clearing back to leave thick belts of timber standing between fields. They had several functions. They would not only have been valuable as shelter belts and field boundaries but would have been essential reserves of timber. Originally they were managed in order to provide a full range of timber. These days they remain in abundance but are seldom exploited for their wood. We often travel within and beside shaws on the walks.

Thus, in the shaws and woods all over the South East, the woodland was managed. Many areas would never have been cleared of trees but were exploited for the timber that was an essential part of the medieval economy. Even by the mid-fourteenth century, little, if any, natural landscape remained in the region, and it would have supported an established network of settlements.

After all this work, there were devastating setbacks from the plagues, and much managed woodland fell into disuse and even re-colonized cleared farmland that the reduced population could no longer maintain.

Since the fourteenth century the changes in the Wealden landscapes have been comparatively minor. Timber continued to be important in the economy, particularly during a period of iron-making which was in its heyday long before the Industrial Revolution took off elsewhere in Britain. This had completely died out by the nineteenth century, but in its time it used massive quantities of timber for fuel. Where forest was cleared, it has long since regenerated.

The story of the woodland on some parts of the Downs is rather different to that of the Weald. It would seem likely that, on much of the clay with flint covering of the western Sussex Downs and the North Downs, the woodland evolved much in the manner already described. However, the eastern area of the South Downs probably developed rather differently — there is a marked contrast between the Downs of east and west to this day.

There has always tended to be a contrast between the development of the high, dry, chalky Downs and the Weald. The Downs attracted the very earliest attention; the Weald was shunned for a long time. This means that the greater part of the drier Downs lost its forest cover much earlier than elsewhere. The woods will have been sparser and easier to clear, and if there is a candidate for very early loss of natural forest cover in the South East, these areas must be it. Perhaps the New Stone Age saw large-scale tillage on this land, for there is considerable human evidence from this time on the Downs.

It becomes clear in the South East that the broad swathes of woodland that appear natural vestiges of an ancient forest have not escaped human action. Some may have seen many successive changes of management and even a number of clearances and regenerations.

See the woodlands for what they are. They are not a natural landscape, but they can, on occasion, give an impression of how the vast forests once were. It is a man-made, hand-built landscape, the end result of centuries of work. That it is beautiful and often haunting and elusive proves it to be a masterpiece of the highest order.

The woodlands of the South East today

The counties of Kent, Sussex and Surrey are among the most heavily wooded in England, with Sussex the leading county with possibly as much as twenty-two per cent of its area wooded.

Nowhere is this density of trees more apparent than in the Greensand country around Haslemere where one can walk for miles with never a glimpse of anything beyond the enclosing woods. There is an overwhelming greenness on the map in the area where Surrey, West Sussex and Hampshire meet.

Looking at all this woodland, it is understandably difficult to believe the frequent complaints by conservationists about the loss of hardwood trees from the landscape – especially since the woodland of the region is predominantly traditional deciduous species in visually superb condition.

The truth is that the woodland we see today is largely an anachronism. We may be the last generation to enjoy traditional English landscapes which in part are made up of woodlands with no contemporary economic use. Sooner or later things with no economic function tend to be replaced by something more useful. This is a harsh judgement on such a thing of beauty as landscape, but it is in general true. Once the fact is grasped, something positive can be done to safeguard the trees.

The woodland in the South East falls into three main categories:

1. Unmanaged or largely unmanaged deciduous woodland.

2. Commercially managed hardwoods (deciduous trees).

3. Commercially managed softwoods (conifers).

It should always be remembered that in the South East 'woodland' refers not just to the large expanses of forest or woods but also to the hedgerows which contain a great deal of timber – especially the Wealden shaws previously mentioned.

Of the three categories defined above, the first is the largest. Once, when timber was an essential commodity, these unmanaged woodlands were a vital economic resource and were maintained accordingly. These days timber is still needed, but the demand has largely shifted away from our own home-grown hardwoods, leaving much of the traditional woodland without a use. Some is conserved for recreation, wildlife or its ascetic value, but the sad truth is that it often remains for no other reason than that it is too much trouble to clear away to make room for other land uses – or it may be situated on land that is of little value if it is cleared. So it is left, degenerating slowly. Some is kept in rough order to provide cover for pheasants for shooting, and incidentally is of considerable value to wildlife. Some woodlands, also, if left completely alone, are able to regenerate themselves in a fairly natural manner and so survive.

But for many unmanaged woodlands – particularly in hedgerows – the writing is on the wall, and while these neglected woodlands may look beautiful, few people realize the sickness that besets them and which will eventually result in their loss from the landscape.

Into the second category there comes an encouragingly large proportion of the South East woodlands. Indeed, the three counties are exceptional in the comparatively large amount of commercially managed deciduous woodland they contain, and I doubt that there is any part of England to compare with the region on this basis. The management takes a number of forms.

In the area south of Haslemere there is a large extent of coppice; a form of woodland management that has all but died out. Where it still exists, it is living history, for the method of coppicing is essentially unchanged since the Middle Ages. It is a treat to encounter it in such abundance in the Surrey and West Sussex borders on our walk. Another area where it is to be seen is on the route between the Medway and Wrotham in Kent.

The coppicing of sweet chestnut leads to a distinctive treescape. Left to themselves, the trees would grow to the full-sized chestnut that is so familiar. However, by cutting the tree at ground level, the roots survive and the stump sprouts a splay of shoots which can be repeatedly cut down on a regular cycle to make stakes, poles and palings. Because there is still a demand for these products, it can be worthwhile for a landowner to commit some of his woodlands to such long-term use – especially on the poor Greensand soils which have very little potential in other directions.

If you happen to be passing at the right time, you may see an area of chestnut coppice being cleared, the timber cut and shaped on site. In a large wood, such as those south of Haslemere, the whole operation can be organized in a cycle so that some areas are being cut whilst others are growing for use in subsequent years. Thus, as you walk through the coppices, dense, dark impenetrable ranks of chestnut soon to be cut will alternate with younger growing shoots and with other areas laid bare by recent harvesting. Where you do obtain a glimpse of a large sweep of coppiced woodland on a distant hillside, the differing heights in the blocks of chestnuts can be clearly seen.

In some areas on the walk I did see large, maturing trees grown in amongst chestnut coppice, with the large trees widely spaced to permit light to the chestnuts beneath. This is 'coppice with standards' and is also medieval in origin, being a system of management that enables the production of both sorts of timber. This was once the prevailing means of woodland management in the Weald.

The other form of hardwood woodland management widely practised is the growing of trees to maturity for felling. Too often felling has meant clearance of trees without replacement – a short-sighted policy which led to a chronic lack of home-produced timber in Britain. True management requires the replacement of the felled timber by planting.

In the region beech and oak are commercially grown, beech particularly on the chalk. The signs of this activity may not be so obvious as in coppiced woodland, except when an area has been wholly cleared. However, there will frequently be noticeboards up beside the path naming the company or estate that manages the woodland – often this will be the Forestry Commission. There may be evidence of the periodic clearing of undergrowth or of trees felled to help the development of those remaining. You may also see areas that are clearly planted in an ordered manner and evidence of the protection of trees against pests – for example fences around young plantations, protective coverings around the bark of saplings, and platforms to shoot deer from set among the trees.

In the western Surrey and West Sussex border areas, timber still has a role to play in the economy. Its abundance means that it is used for jobs where elsewhere alternative materials would be employed. This is particularly so with fencing, and the district has a most attractive profusion of post and rail fences.

Of the third category of commercially managed conifers, the South East does have a certain amount. Everyone knows what these look like, and everyone must have heard the arguments they arouse over their appearance and wildlife sterility. This variety of twentieth-century forestry is comparatively rare in the South East. On the walk there is seen some extensive pine forest on the heaths and a large conifer plantation on the South Downs but little else on these scales. There is room for this land use – there has to be because we need softwoods – as long as it does not swamp everything else.

8

Western Greensand Country

A short section comprising two days' walking, running between the North and South Downs:

Walk 12 Farnham to Haslemere.

Walk 13 Haslemere to South Harting.

Using a base, there are three days' walking:

Walk 13 Farnham to Haslemere. Not a circular walk. A return to Farnham is possible.

Walk 14 Based on Haslemere. A circular walk extending as far south as Maysleith Wood (north-east of Hill Brow).

Walk 15 Based on South Harting. A round trip going northwards to include Rogate.

OS maps required are: 186 Aldershot and Guildford; 197 Chichester and the Downs.

This area offers a contrast to those which precede and follow it and, indeed, offers considerable variation within the area itself. North of Haslemere the Wey Valley is followed as far as Tilford. The route then crosses Greensand heath and woodland, taking in Frensham Little Pond, the Devil's Jumps and the Devil's Punchbowl. There are several good viewpoints included.

South of Haslemere there is almost continuous woodland as far as Rogate. Between Rogate and the South Downs there is a short stretch of Low Weald farmland across the Rother valley and beyond to South Harting.

There are isolated and lonely places on these paths so

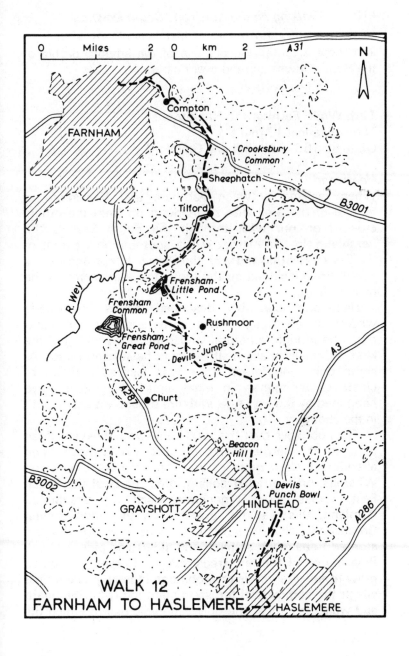

WALK 12
FARNHAM TO HASLEMERE

close to civilization, miles of lush woodlands with here and there a tantalizing glimpse of the smooth profile of the South Downs coming ever nearer.

12th Walk: Farnham to Haslemere
Total distance: 13 miles
OS map: 186 Aldershot and Guildford

Heathland
When walking between Farnham and Haslemere, a feature of the area that so marks it off from the others crossed on our walk through the South East is the heathland. In this district is the southernmost extent of the Surrey Heaths, and with the Devil's Jumps and Devil's Punch Bowl included on the route, these are some of the best of them.

Heathland can be described as a man-made wilderness, for though it has all the appearance of what might be thought a natural landscape, it is nothing of the kind. Originally these heaths would have been forest. At some point the forest cover was lost as a result of clearance by man — in many areas this would have happened by the Iron Age, with fire probably a chief agent in the change.

The poor soils over the sandstones would have yielded little to the farmers and in time would have been abandoned for more rewarding places elsewhere. Whereas, on the richer soils in other parts of the South East, forest could regenerate itself on abandoned farmland, this was not possible on the impoverished Greensand hills. As a result a vegetation of heather, stunted trees (such as birch and alder) and pine evolved. Pine is one of the few trees able to do well enough to grow to full size in this environment. Indeed, it is the pine which the commercial foresters plant today on the heath and which is almost the only economic use to which the land can be put.

Economically unrewarding perhaps but, as a landscape and wildlife habitat, heathland is invaluable. In Surrey, admittedly, the amount of disturbance by walkers, horse-riders and the public generally will have greatly reduced its importance to wildlife. It is the classic land-use conflict – how the public who come to enjoy an area can also unintentionally damage it in the process. Certainly the heaths do look the worse for wear in places; and there is the less obvious problem of the crowds discouraging animals and birds from living in those areas of greatest disturbance, pushing them back into the ever shrinking quiet areas.

What is perhaps more worrying is the decreasing extent of the heaths themselves. The heathland remaining in the South East is but a fraction of what it once was. Much of that remaining is protected in various ways; in fact the Surrey Greensand area is one of the most extensive stretches of protected open space in the South East. Moreover, the Army controls a large part of Surrey heathland, and this can actually help to protect the land from other uses. But the threats are only too obvious as we walk. Commercial forestry has taken large areas, and there is always urbanization looming on the horizon in this region of high population. Fire is a hazard on dry heaths as well.

There is cause for hope. Landscape is a living thing and always changing. What is heathland today could be commercial forest tomorrow. But equally, what is woodland now could be heathland in the future if its tree cover is removed.

In order to get the starting-point of the walk, retrace the steps of the last mile or so of the previous day's walk from Farnham to the bridge over the River Wey at Compton.

Once over the bridge, turn first right down the road to Moor Park College. After some distance the road narrows to a path. Follow this path all the way to a road, where you go right, then immediately left at the road junction just beyond.

Walk along the road and take the first path on the right. When you arrive at a crossroads of paths, go right and proceed up a deeply eroded path to a lane. Walk across the lane and up a drive opposite. Where the drive forks, bear left past Sheephatch Farm. Turn left at the next path junction, which is not signposted. After some distance the path becomes a road. Leave this road by the first path on the right you come to. This path emerges at a road at Tilford, where you should go right, over the River Wey. Then follow the road to the far side of the village green and turn left at the road junction there — just before meeting the Wey again.

Now take the first signposted path on the right, which is a driveway initially and then crosses a garden and comes close to the Wey before heading into woodland.

Turn right at the first track junction you meet, then go straight on at the second.

Note: There is no waymarking of any sort in this area, but the paths themselves are clear enough, and providing the directions here are followed, there should be no problems.

The heather in places beside the path on these higher, drier soils away from the Wey valley is an appetizer for the fine areas of heathland we shall soon be crossing, though much of this former heathland is now thickly afforested with commercial plantations.

When you eventually come to a road, go left, then leave the road and walk down the eastern shore of Frensham Little Pond as far as the south-eastern tip.

From the corner of the pond the path heads off across an area of forestry. When you come to a crossroads of paths, turn right and walk until meeting a road. Go left at the road and proceed along it past a road on the right and as far as a track on the right. Take this track across an area of heathland. There are numerous paths running across here, and the safest option is to follow the broadest of the paths ahead to the prominent humps of the Devil's Jumps. Climb to the top of one of the Jumps from where there is a fine view. It is possible to see the mast on Crooksbury Hill near where the day's walk started. You cannot see the actual line of the route because of the rolling sweep of forest.

The Devil's Jumps

How were these strange hills formed, ranged unexpectedly across the heathland path between Rushmoor and Churt? If you examine the rock exposed on the summit of the Jump, it can be seen to have a darker appearance than the rocks and sands elsewhere on the Greensand hills. Here lies the clue. The Jumps are part of a seam of ironstone that is harder than the crumbly sands all around. Hence, while erosion has worn away the land surface, the harder ironstone has resisted this process to a greater extent than the softer rocks nearby. As a result there is left this little range of hills above the general level of the surrounding land. And because the land towards Farnham is of gentle relief, they serve as a particularly good viewpoint.

The path descending the Jumps is cut into steps like those on the other side used to ascend the hillock. At the foot of the Jumps the path has to be searched for. It runs between wire fences through a small plantation and is slightly to the left of the path down from the Jumps.

When the path meets a road, turn left. Go left at the first road junction and then immediately right. Once on this last road, follow it for a mile until beyond the name sign on the outskirts of the village of Pitch Place. Once past this name sign, walk on until there is a sharp left-hand bend in the road. At this bend turn right onto an unsignposted track in front of a house called Little Pitch.

This track narrows to a path, deeply cut and overhung

by trees with farmland to either side – about the only area of farmland passed between the Wey valley and Haslemere. Keep walking until you meet a lane. At this lane turn right, go 50 yards and then turn left down an unmarked path that is narrow and ill defined at first, though once located it becomes clear and easy to follow. It is now a gentle climb through woodland. When you meet a woodland ride, turn right and continue uphill, following the line of the overhead power cables here. (This sounds awful, I know, but they really are small, inconspicuous pylons!)

At the next junction, go right. Now, over to the left are views across the Devil's Punch Bowl. Go left at the next path junction.

The Devil's Punch Bowl

In common with other curious and long unexplained landforms, this has attracted the idea that the Devil was responsible. This is unlikely, because he was probably too busy leaping about on his Jumps and making bread in his Kneading Trough.

The Punch Bowl is the head of a valley. The stream has cut down through the sandstone to the clay beneath. Water can drain through the sandstone but is stopped by the clays below and emerges at the surface as springs. It is the erosion of these springs that has undermined and steepened the sides of the Punch Bowl to turn it into a large landscape feature instead of the normal insignificant head of a valley. We do not get the best view of the Punch Bowl. For this, divert eastwards to where the A3 swings around the head of the Bowl.

The last view of the Punch Bowl is from below the car-park at Hindhead. Go through the car-park and leave by its main entrance to meet the A3. Opposite, and slightly to the right of, the entrance, on the other side of the road is a path. Take this path. Stay on this path across an area of heathland that offers the best viewpoint of the day's walk on its high Greensand position.

Note: There are numerous bridlepaths and footpaths criss-crossing this heath. Keep to the main one. Eventually it drops into woodland.

When you meet a track near a group of houses, turn right. This track then becomes a metalled road and can be followed all the way into Haslemere.

Haslemere
Accommodation: There is a good range of accommodation in the Haslemere area.

Public Transport: The area is very well served by public transport – both trains and bus. Moreover, as it is a one-way walk from Farnham to Haslemere, the bus services between Farnham and Haslemere are of particular value to those needing to return to a base.

Parking: This should present no problem in Haslemere.

13th Walk: Haslemere to South Harting
Total distance: 14 miles
OS maps: 186 Aldershot and Guildford and 197 Chichester and The Downs

Stage 1: Haslemere to Maysleith Wood
The starting-point of the walk is at Hammer, to the west of Haslemere. If not wishing to walk, it is possible to catch a bus out to this point. These way-finding instructions read from the B2131 roundabout at GR 882323.

Walk from this roundabout onto the minor road that goes off south towards Kingsley Green. Once on this road, walk only a short distance and then turn first right onto a track. Go past the signposted path on the left and follow the track until it turns sharp right. Here, go straight ahead on a path and leave the track.

When you meet a road, go right. Bear right at the next

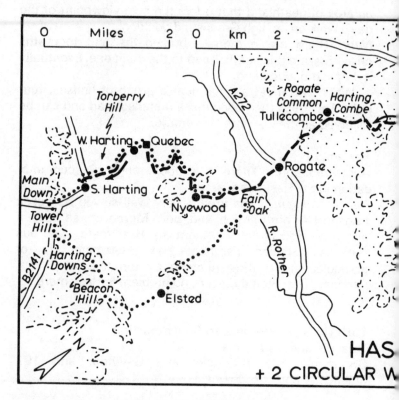

junction. When this road turns sharply into the gates of a house, go straight ahead along a signposted path into the woods. From here there are miles of walking with hardly a glimpse beyond the trees.

Once on this path, walk past one other path joining it and then go left at the path beyond, over a stile. Then cross a field and make the most of the views to the South Downs and of Telegraph Hill in the middle distance before plunging back into the woods at the far corner of the field.

Now descend the hill through the woods, crossing a bridlepath *en route*, and go right at the next signposted path. Then turn first left and then first right. This last path

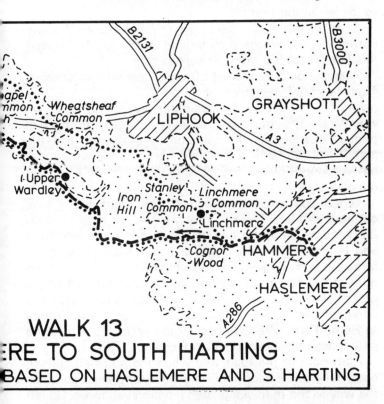

Wheatsheaf
Common
apel
nmon
h
Upper
Wardley
B2131
LIPHOOK
GRAYSHOTT
B3000
A3
Stanley
Iron
Hill Common
Linchmere
Common
Linchmere
Linchmere
Cognor
Wood
HAMMER
HASLEMERE
A286

WALK 13
RE TO SOUTH HARTING
BASED ON HASLEMERE AND S. HARTING

comes out as a track to Linchmere Cottage. At the end of the drive to the cottage you encounter another track. Walk straight across it onto a path in the woods opposite. You then come out at a road. Turn right, then first left beside Newlands Cottage.

Follow this route to the next signposted path in front of a house. Here, you should take the path around to the right for 150 yards to a rough track, where you turn left. A little further on there is another signposted junction where you should go left.

Bear left at the next fork. Then, at the signposted junction beyond, go straight on – the path bending around to the left at this point.

Stay on this path, ignoring one joining from the left. Further on, follow the path around to the left at the next junction. There is a signpost here to help.

Pass the path on the left 50 yards beyond this junction. There is a brief view here.

Note: It can be very disconcerting walking in unknown woodland. The profusion of ever-changing unmapped paths, rides and tracks can add to problems, and the inability to see familiar landmarks beyond the woods can be worrying. Follow these instructions and you will get out alive!

When you arrive at the next path, opposite a lone cottage, turn left. There is a view to the left here towards Blackdown. The route has now emerged from woodland and is entering an area with a considerable amount of farmland. Go right when you come to a road and then right at the first road junction you meet. Turn left at the next. Follow this road until it makes a sharp left-hand bend, where you should go straight on down a farm road to Home Farm. Walk on past Home Farm, go across the path crossroads beyond and proceed to a road.

Turn right at the road, and when the metalled surface ends, take a left-hand fork on a track, and keep going all the way to the third signposted junction you meet. Go left here, along a stony track, until it meets a road, where you turn right.

Take the first left off this road. This is a drive, and after 50 yards you should bear left. At the next path junction, go straight on through a farmyard and continue ahead at the junction beyond. The way is signposted at intervals, but in places the path is rather indistinct, so when the path begins to make right-angle turns in Maysleith Wood, take care to use the signs for guidance. Doing so will bring you to a farm, and you should pass this down the track to a lane.

Stage 2: Maysleith Wood to Nyewood

Go left at this road and then turn first right on a signposted public footpath. The footpath runs beside a small lake and then heads through woodland on a path that is vague in parts but waymarked with point blobs on trees in places. On emerging from the woods, there is a stile and a footpath signpost. Cross the stile and head straight across the field to a road. Ignore the footpath going off to the right.

Turn right at the road. Walk for about a third of a mile, then turn left onto the first signposted bridleway you come to (beside an entrance to Fyning Hill Estate). The walking is now along a broad, clear ride with signposts at intervals to help. Pass any paths or rides off to either side – these are generally marked as private in any case.

The path eventually comes out to another road. Cross the road to a path on the other side and walk down this path until you meet a road at Halecommon. On the way do not turn off to either side. Go left at the road and follow it into Rogate.

From Rogate there is a crossing of a typical piece of Low Weald country to South Harting at the foot of the South Downs. It can be seen on the map that there is a direct walk by road to South Harting and in very wet conditions (or very tired conditions!) this will prove the best alternative. The route of this stage described below is less direct.

Cross the A272 in Rogate and walk down the road past the church and follow it all the way to Nyewood, a distance of about $1\frac{1}{2}$.

Stage 3: Nyewood to South Harting

In Nyewood walk to the far end of the village and take a footpath on the right just before reaching a bus-shelter. If you go as far as the post office, you have missed the path.

Just after you have joined it, the path forks. Bear right

here. There is a signpost soon after the fork to confirm the route. Once past the signpost, follow the path around to the right. There are several little paths off to either side in the woods which should be ignored.

You will come to a point where the clear path being followed turns a sharp left-hand 90° angle across a small water channel. Take care not to divert onto one of the other paths branching off at this point.

Keep walking until you come to a bridlepath gate marked 'Private Woodland'. Do not go through, but turn right here and after 50 yards you reach the edge of the woods and leave them by way of a stile. There is a footpath signpost here. Go straight across a field to a signpost visible on its far side. Once there, go left along the hedgerow. Proceed into the next field and leave it over a stile. Then walk along a hedgerow straight ahead to a wire fence. Then go in a diagonal across the next field to a stile and signpost on its other side. Go over the stile and turn left along the hedge. Follow this hedge to an area of wire fence before the hedgerow is resumed again. Where the hedgerow is resumed, the path turns left over a stile. Once over, turn right across a field. Take care on this part of the route, for there are no footpaths worn on the ground. The line of the path is uphill to a gate visible on the brow of a hill.

Once on this hill brow there is a path junction, where you should go ahead on a clear track to Hill Ash Farm. When you come to a lane, turn right, and then left at the first road junction you meet and walk into West Harting.

At a road junction on the other side of West Harting, turn left. Once on this road, take the first footpath on the right that you come to. Follow this path all the way to the B2141. Although passing very close to Torberry Hill here, it is an unremarkable feature from this position. By far the best view is gained from the South Downs behind Harting.

Cross the B2141 and enter a metalled farm road opposite. Just before reaching the farm buildings, take a

Ranmore Common, Surrey.
The church spire is a familiar
landmark to walkers in the
Dorking area

The River Wey near Shalford

Shere: an attractive Surrey village in a trim and leafy countryside

Above: Crossing the River Wey at Tilford on the walk from Farnham to Haslemere

Below left: The vantage point of the Devil's Jumps gives a wide view of the heathland near Frensham

Below right: Coppiced woodland near Haslemere: the foreground shows the cut and stacked palings, in the distance the chestnut coppice from which the palings were cut

View west from Beacon Hill towards Hampshire, South Harting in the middle distance

Arundel town and castle: a base for many walks on the nearby South Downs

Springhead Hill in winter

Burpham, an isolated village in the Arun Valley

Chanctonbury Ring seen from the path which links it with Cissbury Ring

View west along the South Downs scarp above Poynings

Devil's Dyke: this dry valley is one of the best known Sussex landmarks

Alfriston, East Sussex: a picturesque and popular village in a beautiful area

The mysterious Long Man of Wilmington viewed from Wilmington village

The South Downs from Windover Hill, the furthest hill is Firle Beacon

path on the left which leads to a minor road. Go left on this road into South Harting.

Circular walk based on Haslemere
Total distance: 14 miles
OS map: 186 Aldershot and Guildford
The furthest extent of this walk is Maysleith Wood near Rake. Therefore, for the outward part of the round trip read Stage 1 of the Haslemere to South Harting walk.

Stage 2: Maysleith Wood to Hammer
Turn right at the road, and then turn first right on a signposted path. You now climb for some way up a deeply eroded path. At one point to the right there is a glimpse of the South Downs with Cocking chalk quarries standing out clearly. Turn left at the first path junction you come to and walk to the A3. Cross the A3 and go ahead down a broad metalled road which becomes unsurfaced after some way.

At the first junction you meet, take the second turning on the right which is a broad forestry track. Go straight on at the next junction, and you are now on a narrower path. At the next path junction there is a signpost. Go right here. In places there are patches of heathland in open areas within the woods. Go straight on at the next junction. This path then joins a track that leads to the A3 again.

Go left at the A3 past the Black Fox Inn and then right, down a lane on the right-hand side of the A3 at a bend. This minor road then meets another, where you should go ahead up a track. Walk straight ahead at the next three path junctions you come to. Beyond these the track forks, and you should take the left-hand fork. Again, proceed straight ahead at the next two path junctions. In this way the path eventually meets a track where you should bear left and follow it straight ahead to a road. Turn left at the road, walk uphill to a road junction and turn right. Now take the first path on the right, which is signposted.

Follow this path around to the left at the next path junction. The path then ascends a rise to meet a track, where you should go straight ahead, following the signpost. Turn right at the next junction. Walk on past a path on the right and then turn left at the next signposted junction. Go straight ahead at the next junction, and turn right at the next two junctions beyond. After the last junction there is a path on the right 50 yards on, which is to be ignored.

Walk straight on at the next two path junctions. After the second junction the path skirts a field on the edge of woodland and then emerges to continue across a field beside its right-hand boundary. This comes out at a road in Linchmere, where you should go left, then first right.

Now turn first right down a signposted track. Go straight on at the next three path junctions. When you meet a road, go straight ahead. Keep on ahead at the next junction, and then turn left at the one beyond.

On meeting a track, continue ahead along it and walk as far as a road. Turn left at the road and follow it back to the roundabout at Hammer, from where you can return to Haslemere.

Circular Walk based on South Harting
Total distance: 10 miles
OS map: 197 Chichester and The Downs

Stage 1: South Harting to Beacon Hill
See Stage 1 of the South Harting to Cocking walk.

Stage 2: Beacon Hill to Rother Vale
Descend the eastern side of Beacon Hill and take the first path on the left. This is the route down the scarp. As you go down through the woods, cross one bridlepath and pass a turning on the right a little further on. Leaving the

woods, there is a junction of paths. Go left here, through a gate, and down a track enclosed by high banks.

Go left, then immediately right at the next path junction. Continue to a road, where you should proceed ahead to the crossroads in Elsted. Walk straight over the crossroads down a No Through Road as far as the church. At the church take the second path on the right, which is up a set of steps in the church wall in front of a farmyard gateway.

Leave the churchyard over the rear wall. Once in the field on the far side of the wall, follow a wire fence around to the left. You will then see a signpost and should go across the field along a track to a hedge where there is a stile. Go across the stile, through a belt of woodland and across a field to a signpost visible on its far side.

Follow the path through an area of rough semi-woodland and across the corner of a field to another stile and signpost.

Note: Whilst great trouble has been taken over waymarking and stile-construction on these paths from Elsted, they are obviously under-used and slightly overgrown in places – though are nowhere impassable.

Go in a diagonal across the next field to a stile, and once over it turn left across a field towards the middle of the left-hand hedgerow. There is a stile and signpost in this hedge, and you should follow its directions along the centre of a shaw. Although the path itself is indistinct, there are stiles at intervals to mark its direction through the timbered field boundary. Eventually the path leaves the shaw by way of a stile and goes across two fields. In the third field walk beside the right-hand fence, uphill, to a road. Turn right on the road, then go first left on a path which runs between high banks for some distance.

When this path meets a track, turn left and follow the track all the way to a road. At this point there is a choice. It is possible to turn right and walk into Rogate (this is only worthwhile if wishing to have lunch at one of the

Rogate pubs) or to turn left and begin the return trip.

If you go into Rogate, it is necessary to return to this point for the final stage of the walk. Turn left and follow the road to Nyewood.

Stage 3: Nyewood to South Harting
See Stage 3 of the Haslemere to South Harting walk.

9

The South Downs
West of the Arun

This part of the walk covers the South Downs between South Harting and the River Arun. There are two days walking:

Walk 14 South Harting to Cocking.
Walk 15 Cocking to Arundel.

There are three circular walks:

Walk 16 Based on Cocking. A westwards round-trip extending as far as Beacon Hill above East Harting.

Walk 17 Using Cocking as the base. An eastwards round-trip travelling as far as Littleton Down.

Walk 18 Based on Arundel. A circular walk going westwards as far as Stane Street (between Burton Down and Bignor Hill).

The OS map needed is: 197 Chichester and The Downs.

A quiet, rather remote corner of Sussex full of attractive woodland and farmland and offering several long-distance views in all directions.

The walks follow the scarp, explore the dip slope on the southern backs of the Downs and also venture out onto the land at the northern foot of the scarp. In addition the Arun valley is followed for some way.

All very picturesque and peaceful and not a heavily used path in the whole area.

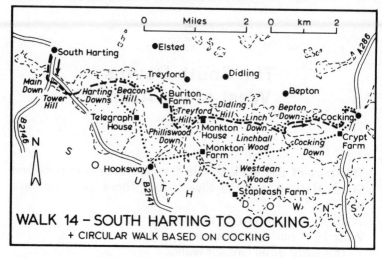

WALK 14 – SOUTH HARTING TO COCKING
+ CIRCULAR WALK BASED ON COCKING

14th Walk: South Harting to Cocking
Total distance: 8 miles
OS map: 197 Chichester and The Downs.

South Harting
Accommodation: Reasonable amount of accomodation.
Public Transport: Served by bus.
Parking: In roads only.

Stage 1: South Harting to Beacon Hill
Leave South Harting beside the B2146 on a rather dangerous stretch along the edge of the road past the 'Coach and Horses'. Take the first minor road off to the right once past this pub. The road ends after a short distance, at which point you should continue ahead on a footpath. Simply stay on this path, ignoring any junctions off to either side, and walk up the scarp of the South Downs until you meet the B2146 below Main Down. Go straight across the road, having now joined the South

Downs Way, and walk along the path until it meets the B2146. Go straight across here, and the path now comes out on the open downland of Harting Downs. Now follow the clear waymarking up onto Beacon Hill.

Stage 2: Beacon Hill to Cocking
Walk down the eastern side of Beacon Hill. At the foot of the hill, paths go off in several directions — take the middle of the five paths, straight ahead onto the next hill.

On the far side of this hill there is another junction of paths, where you should go right. Keep straight on at the junction of paths about 150 yards beyond. Go straight on at the one after this. The path comes to a track in the vicinity of Buriton Farm. Turn left here and then first right. The track now winds up onto Philliswood Down. Go straight on at the path junction part-way up the hill.

Turn left at the next junction. Walk along this path through the woodland. On the very edge of the woodland, just as the trees end, the Devil's Jumps are over to the left of the path. They need to be looked for, otherwise it is easy to go past.

The walking is now easy as far as wayfinding is concerned. You can virtually put away the map and forget about it for several miles and just follow the clear track of the ridgeway path ahead. The South Downs are full of such straightforward paths.

Walk in this manner until approaching Cocking Down. Here, go left at the path crossroads at GR856170 — in other words, the second crossroads after passing the triangulation station on Linch Down.

This path now goes down the scarp below, and you should follow it all the way to the vicinity of Crypt Farm, passing a path from the left *en route* on Bepton Down. Near Crypt Farm you meet a farm track. Turn left here and follow it to a road. Go right at the road and walk into Cocking.

Cocking
Accommodation: This is lacking, but in view of the accessibility of the village from Chichester and Midhurst, it is not a problem.
Public transport: Buses to Chichester and Midhurst.
Parking: No car-parks, but there is the odd kerbside place available in Cocking.

Circular walk based on Cocking (westwards)
Total distance: 13 miles
OS map: 197 Chichester and The Downs.

Stage 1: Cocking to Beacon Hill
Leave Cocking by walking along beside the A286 until about 200 yards beyond Cocking Stores. At this point, on the right-hand side of the A286, there is a rough track going off signposted as a public footpath. Go past this turning and take the next right, which is a road labelled as 'Unsuitable for motor vehicles' and which has a footpath signpost a few yards down the lane. Now go on down this road to Crypt Farm.

As you go through the buildings of Crypt Farm, pass a stables on the left and just beyond them take a signposted footpath that goes uphill on the left. The path goes up through woodland. Keep straight on and it then leaves the woods to follow a field boundary as it climbs up towards Cocking Down.

When you arrive at a point where the field boundary bends away to the left, strike out across the open field uphill, following the line of a wire fence. The path here is indistinct. Having taken this course, you will met a gate and signpost. Go straight on here, across the next field, and the path meets the South Downs Way. Go straight across the Way on a path heading towards Newfarm Plantation.

The path passes through a short stretch of woodland and then emerges into the open again. Take the second path on the left down a broad, grassy ride between conifers. There are excellent views from here as far as the Isle of Wight.

After about 400 yards, another ride crosses the path. Turn right here. There is a signpost here to help, but it has to be searched for – so it is not much use really. Now that you are in the dense conifer forest take care to follow the map and written notes carefully. Use a compass if necessary.

Go straight across the first ride that crosses the path. This is met after about 150 yards. Go straight on at the next two rides you meet. The path then goes down into a hollow. Go across the ride running through the hollow and straight ahead up the slope on the other side. Ignore the two paths coming in from the right on the way up the slope. Eventually you come to a junction of five paths with a signpost. Turn left here (Note: this is the second path on the left, not the first left at this multiple junction). You now enter the beech woodland of Westdean Woods. Follow the path across a track and stay on it, ignoring any paths that join it. The path comes to an area of open woodland with a nature reserve to the left. When you come to a second nature reserve notice board, a narrow path forks off right. Take this. (If you come to a building in the woods before meeting this narrow path, you have missed the junction by a short distance and will need to retrace your steps.)

The enclosed path gradually opens out and leaves the woods behind. Go right at a road and walk along to the road junction at Stapleash Farm, where you go right. Follow the road until just around a sharp left-hand bend, where you should take a signposted path on the right. Now follow this track all the way to Monkton Farm. At the Monkton Farm buildings, turn left up the hillside. The path is signposted beside the gate leading to the old farm

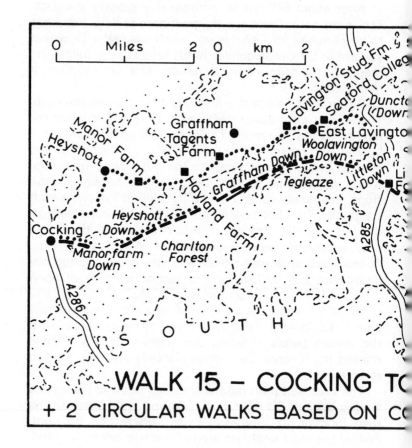

WALK 15 – COCKING TO
+ 2 CIRCULAR WALKS BASED ON C

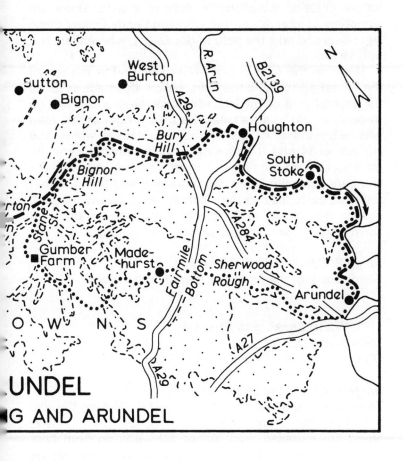

buildings. Keep the wire fence to the left for the first 50 yards up the hill, then cross over it by means of a stile, continuing to follow the fence on its other side.

At the top of the field, cross over a stile and go ahead with a hedge to the right. The path then crosses the fields before entering woodland by way of a gate. There are signposts at intervals on the woodland path. Follow these signposts and take the path to Hooksway, where there is a pub for lunch.

Walk up the road out of Hooksway, and at the top of the hill take a track on the right. Follow this track as far as the second path on the left, where you cross a stile and go through a field to a metalled road. Turn right at this road and walk along it past Telegraph House, where the surface ends and it becomes a track. Beyond here the track forks – go right here. A short distance beyond there is a gate across the path. Go through it and then turn left onto the path, leaving the clearest track. Follow the path around the bottom of Beacon Hill until you are onto the Downs crest. Here go right, up onto Beacon Hill.

Stage 2: Beacon Hill to Cocking
See Stage 2 of the South Harting to Cocking walk.

15th Walk: Cocking to Arundel
Total distance: 15 miles
OS map: 197 Chichester and The Downs

Stage 1: Cocking to Littleton Down
To leave Cocking, take the minor road to Cocking Church. Just past the church the road branches. Go left here, along the metalled road. About 50 yards on from here there is a stile and footpath signpost in the hedge on the right. Cross this stile. The path now goes through the field beyond in a rough diagonal to a stile on the far side. The path is invisible on the ground.

In the second field turn right and follow the field boundary uphill towards the woods. Go through the woods and out onto Manorfarm Down. The path uphill on Manorfarm Down is invisible, but if you go in a left-hand diagonal, all should be well. Once across the first field, there is a stile and signpost to help direction-finding. At the far side of the second field you will meet the broad track of the South Downs Way, where you should turn left. Although the views are good from Manorfarm Down, for much of the way to Littleton Down the path is set just back from the crest of the hills and is often in woods, so the view is just occasionally glimpsed to the north.

At first the Way is of track width, but it narrows to a path further on. Few directions are necessary now. The path is clear, easy to follow and well signposted; do not take any paths off to either side. Follow the map until you come out onto Littleton Down, having walked about $3\frac{1}{2}$-4 miles since joining the South Downs Way at Manorfarm Down.

When you come out of the trees at the top of Littleton Down, the path goes downhill through two fields to meet a farm track.

Stage 2: Littleton Down to Stane Street
Follow the farm track ahead to the A285, where you should go right, then immediately left onto a clear track. Follow this track all the way up to Burton Down, passing any private tracks that join from either side.

Go straight ahead at the path junction on Burton Down. The next path met after this is Stane Street.

Stage 3: Stane Street to Arundel
Turn left on meeting Stane Street, and then go right at the broad path running along the crest of the Downs. There are numerous tracks and paths in this area, but there is signposting to help. Follow the South Downs Way as it sweeps clearly up onto Bignor Hill, past an area of rough

parking.

Descending the other side of Bignor Hill, the track goes down into a hollow between Bignor and Westburton Hills. There is a junction of paths here, where you should go right past some barns and up clearly onto Westburton Hill.

Continue to follow the Way off Westburton Hill towards the A29. Go straight on at the path junction near Bury Hill. Just beyond here the track divides into three. Any of these can be taken, as they all meet up at the A29.

Turn right at the A29, then go first left after about 100 yards. Again, this track is easy to follow and leads clearly to a road outside Houghton. Turn right at the road and follow it to the B2139 running through Houghton. Turn right, then immediately left at this road, down South Lane. The lane runs between a few houses then becomes a track and in turn emerges on the west bank of the River Arun.

From here the route into Arundel follows the river all the way, but there are a number of minor diversions that need clarifying. It is easy enough to follow the path as it goes beside the big loop of the Arun opposite North Stoke. When it reaches the far side of the woods on this section of the route, a gate bars the way. Go through this and follow the fence ahead along the edge of a field with a thin band of woodland on the left beside the Arun. On the far side of the field, a track goes ahead, skirting the edge of the trees above the river, and leads to South Stoke.

In South Stoke pass through a farmyard to a road, where you turn left. The road becomes a track beyond the church and leads down to beside the river, where you turn right and follow the embankment path. It is now very straightforward walking beside the Arun as far as the Black Rabbit Inn near Offham. At this point walk along in front of the inn as far as the road at its far end. Turn left off the road to rejoin the embankment path.

Take the path as far as the far side of the wildfowl

reserve. Where the fence ends near the sluice, follow the signposted footpath to the right as far as a road. Turn left at the road and use the left-hand roadside footpath to follow the road into Arundel.

Arundel
Accommodation: This is plentiful.
Public transport: Served by bus and a railway station.
Parking: Extensive

Circular walk based on Cocking (eastwards)
Total distance: 12 miles
OS map: 197 Chichester and The Downs

Stage 1: Cocking to Littleton Down
This is the outward section of the walk. See Stage 1 of the Cocking to Arundel walk.

Stage 2: Littleton Down to Cocking
On meeting the farm track at the foot of Littleton Down, turn left. This is a broad earth track. About 100 yards after passing the track to Dogkennel Cottages, the path divides. Turn right here; it is clearly waymarked.

Go straight ahead at the next path junction. The path is invisible as it crosses the field, but follow the contour of the slope around, bearing slightly left, and you will come to a stile on the far side of the field. It is signposted at this point, and the path goes through a wooded area to meet a rough road serving a quarry. Turn right here and follow the road down to the A285, where you should go left. Walk for a short distance beside the A285 as far as the lay-by at the view point on Duncton Down.

On the left-hand (uphill) side of the lay-by, a footpath goes off into the woods. Take this, and then turn left at the next signposted junction of paths. A hundred yards on from here, a path goes off to the right. It is unmarked by any waymarking and a little overgrown, but it is the one to take. Care is needed to find it, but after the first section it soon becomes clearer and easy to follow as it goes down the scarp slope through the woods.

At the foot of the slope the path comes out at a house. Turn left here and you meet a road, where you should go left. Follow the road until it ends. At this point turn right on a private road through the gates of Seaford College. Follow the road around to the left beside a fence. From here it is simple route-finding. Follow the private road, ignoring all junctions of paths or other private roads, until you meet the public road near the church at Graffham.

Walk along the road past the church to a point where there are two left-hand turnings close together. Take the second left, a surfaced road leading to Tagents Farm. In front of the farm continue on ahead down a green lane, going straight on at the first path crossroads.

The green lane goes for some way and then turns suddenly left. Stay alert after this turn, for a little further on the actual path to follow goes sharp right and leaves the green lane. There is a footpath signpost at this point, but without care it could be missed. Having turned right, cross a stile, and go through the field beyond along the right-hand field boundary. At the other side of the field, cross a stile in the fence on the right and maintain the same direction along beside the field boundary.

Go straight ahead at the next path crossroads. It is signposted here and, as a check on direction, Hayland Farm should be over to the right. The path ahead is invisible, but keep on ahead in a straight line until you strike the edge of an area of woodland projecting out into the large field. The path goes through the woodland to emerge on the far side beside a copse. Follow the right-hand fence around to the right behind the copse to meet a gate on a farm track. Go through the gate and along the track as far as a farm road.

Turn left at the road and follow it through Manor Farm

to come out at a corner of a lane. Go straight ahead and through the village of Heyshott until just past the church. Turn left at the road junction beyond the church.

Follow this road as far as the next junction, where you should turn right and follow the lane back into Cocking.

Circular walk based on Arundel (westwards)
Total distance: 14 miles
OS map: 197 Chichester and The Downs.

Stage 1: Arundel to Stane Street
The best way to leave Arundel is to go first to the easily located cathedral. Approaching the cathedral from the direction of the castle along London Road, you will come to a turning that goes downhill on the left in front of the cathedral. This road is called Parsons Hill. Go down it and turn right at the bottom of the road and walk as far as a roundabout on the edge of the town.

Walk across the roundabout and go over to the A27 exit, signposted for Chichester. At the point where the A27 comes onto the roundabout, there is a private road on the right-hand side between two converted gate-houses. Go down here and then take a path on the left immediately past the houses which goes up into the woods.

Go right at the next path junction, and then straight ahead at the crossroads afterwards. About 200 yards on from here there is another path junction, where you should take the right fork. Take this path, crossing a stile *en route*, and walk as far as the next signposted path junction. Here go straight on, but bear slightly right to avoid taking the rough path ahead into the woods by mistake.

The route now climbs up out of the woods, and the path runs between fences across open fields once it leaves the trees behind. Having crossed the fields, you come to another path junction where you should go left. The track now runs along the edge of woods and eventually enters them. It is almost impossible to take a wrong turning off the track, for those joining it from either side all have 'private' notices on.

Once you have crossed most of Sherwood Rough, the path comes to a large, triangular-shaped clearing where a track and a ride meet. Go straight ahead here for 50 yards along the stony track and then bear right up a path through the trees. It is signposted and goes slightly uphill.

At the top of the slope there is a gate, stile and signpost. Cross the stile and walk a further 50 yards and then bear left. You are now walking on a section of a nature trail. At the next junction of paths turn right, following the nature trail arrows. Follow the nature trail posts along the edge of a field into an area of woodland ahead. From here the path is unclear, but keep the A29 to your left and walk until meeting a car-park and small roadside café.

In front of the café is a footpath signpost. Go over the A29 and follow its direction down a path on the far side of the road. Go straight ahead at the first two path junctions. After crossing a stile, the path begins to climb out of Fairmile Bottom up the hill to Madehurst. The path is invisible on the ground, but simply go up the hill following the hedge boundary towards a house on the hilltop ahead.

At Madehurst walk straight ahead as far as a road. Turn right at the road and walk along it. Then turn first left down a private road to New Barn Farm. Go straight ahead at the crossroads at the foot of the private road. Now go uphill on the road until almost at the hilltop, where a signpost points left just beyond a cottage on the right.

Two hundred yards after turning left, two tracks meet the road. There is a signpost here, and it should be followed along the second track, leaving the road behind.

Continue down the track, ignoring any turn-offs. When you come to within sight of a wall and stable just ahead and are standing on a bend in the track, you will be at a junction. There is a track coming in from the left here, but you want a path on the right, indicated through a field by a slightly hidden signpost. (Note: If you walk as far as the stable and barn, you have missed the path.)

Go across the field towards a wide gap in the trees on the far side. Once at the gap, go through a gate and then go right, along the wire fence beyond, following the footpath signposts. The path skirts around the edge of woodland beside a wire fence. All being well, you should be able to see the twin masts on Burton Down in the right-hand distance. If not, panic!

Go straight on at the next path crossroads, and turn right at the junction 50 yards beyond. Go straight on at the next path junction, and then bear left at the fork in the area of Great Down.

On meeting a track, turn right and follow this route up to Gumber Farm, through the farmyard and on to meet Stane Street. Do not expect anything too impressive on the ground at Stane Street, but since it is possible to look right along its line to the spire of Chichester Cathedral, it is hardly unimpressive either. The higher elevation and lack of enclosing woodland mean that there are now views over some distance.

Follow the path past the first two paths on the right that you pass. Just beyond the second path junction, a gate bars the way. Go slightly uphill and to the left at this point to meet a stile and signpost. Follow the arm ahead that indicates Stane Street. The next junction you meet is with the South Downs Way, and from here begins the return leg.

Stage 2: Stane Street to Arundel
See Stage 3 of the Cocking to Arundel walk. (For the first direction, go straight on instead of turning left.)

10
Prehistoric Landmarks
of the South Downs

The South Downs are rich in prehistoric remnants, many of them clearly discernible to the casual observer. It is important that these ancient monuments are not seen in isolation – they may be all that is obviously left from these times, but they should be viewed as fragments left over from a more complex picture. In other words, they should be seen in the context of remains from a whole landscape; the full extent of that former landscape's development is still uncertain.

The time-span of human prehistory is far greater than that of recorded history, so it is a period of different races, cultures and innovations – and the types of relic vary accordingly. Why should the South Downs be so prolific in such remains? It is probably a mixture of two key factors. Firstly, the South Downs were attractive to early man – they offered easier soils to work than the Weald; the woodland was probably easier to clear for agriculture; they could provide a communication route, and they gave the security of high ground – so they attracted the earliest settlement. Secondly, until very recently the Downs had been only minimally disturbed by later land uses. They were under grass for a long time, and thus the monuments were well preserved. Sadly, this is no longer the case.

Neolithic times
'Causewayed camps'
These belong to an early neolithic period, and their original function is a mystery. They are one of a number of varieties of hilltop earthwork visited on the walks, and not to be confused with others. There are four on the South Downs, and we pass very close to two of them – at Barkhale (Bignor Hill) and Coombe Hill (Jevington). They are not spectacular earthworks and can be unclear. They are roughly circular with rings of banks and ditches and causeways crossing these barriers; hence the name.

Long barrows
These are a familiar sight, but not to be confused with burial mounds of later periods. The results of weather, farming, Victorian amateur archaeologists and sheer antiquity can blur the differences between the types of barrow and even make the mound itself indistinct. About a dozen exist on the South Downs. It seems they were reserved for a few special burials. Some of the earthen mounds are up to 200 feet long. They are to be seen between the Adur and Beachy Head, together with other, later works.

Flint mines
Flint can be taken for the asking from the surface all over the Downs but it was mined in order to exploit the best veins of material (many of the mines were still worked as late as the Bronze Age). There are several sites on the Downs showing as grown-over pits and spoil heaps. The associated axe industry concentrated on the 'secondary escarpment' south of the main Downs crest where folding of the rock had left good unweathered flint accessible. Cissbury is an example visited on the walk – one of the most famous in Britain. We shall also pass near Windover Hill at Wilmington.

Bronze Age
Round Barrows

Not all the dead of the Bronze Age were buried in round barrows. Even so, there are about a thousand in Sussex, all but fifty of them on the Downs. We walk past them in massive quantities, although many are little more than remarkable lumps. Nevertheless, enough remain clearly visible to give an impression of their former shape.

Round barrows have a variety of shapes, often grouped together in cemeteries of different types. Often the top is sunken due to internal collapse or interference by 'treasure-hunters' in the past. They are particularly thick on the ground in the area between the Arun and Adur, on Plumpton Plain and in the Firle Beacon area. But far from all this, on Treyford Hill, west of the Arun, are the Devil's Jumps (not to be confused with the Surrey Heath Jumps) which we visit. These are a well-preserved series of barrows, quiet on the edge of a wood.

'Cross dykes', 'cross ridge dykes' or 'covered ways'.

These probably had a range of functions, depending on location. Differences between the varieties of use may have become blurred over time. Today they appear as sunken tracks or ditches. Some were droveways – no doubt use did much to deepen them. Sullington Hill and Barnsfarm Hill, both near Washington, are examples. Some were probably the property boundaries of ranches or farms, as at Belle Tout near Birling Gap. There are numerous later hollowed tracks on the Downs – the genuine article may be less clear.

Iron Age
Hill forts

Barrow building was not practised in this period, and the main legacy of this time is the hill fort. Dramatically situated on hilltops, they are a most striking feature, and we visit a number of them – not least because they are often on the finest viewpoints. Some were mere stock enclosures with low banks, but others clearly had a defensive role with a prominent position, deep ditches and high banks that would once have been surmounted by timber ramparts.

We visit Cissbury and Wolstonbury Hill; both very impressive sites. On the far west Downs we look upon the isolated Torbery Hill fort north of the Downs at Harting while standing on the ramparts of Beacon Hill.

Lynchets

Some term these 'Celtic fields', but it is an inaccurate term. The South Downs were once full of these early field patterns 'fossilized' beneath the grassland. Twentieth-century arable farming has ploughed a great many into oblivion. However, many do remain, and some are probably much earlier than the Iron Age. They appear as steps or terraces on hillsides, being small and rectangular in shape and separated from one another by banks. (The actual field is the flat part of the step; the drop down to the next field is the bank.) The banks were created by the wash of soil downhill and also the ploughing pushing the earth the same way – it therefore led to an accumulation of material on the downslope side of the field.

Two places where they can still be seen are Coombe Hill near Jevington and Windover Hill near Wilmington. They are clearest in low, slanting evening light when shadows clarify the shape. A great deal also depends upon the angle from which they are approached.

The fact that these early farmers had to use such slopes suggests that these fields are but remnants of a once more extensive farmscape, the full extent of which has vanished under centuries of later agriculture in more used areas.

As to the mysterious Long Man of Wilmington, its origins are unknown. The original chalk figure has been greatly altered and interfered with over the years. Its age is unknown, but it could well be very old. Whatever the truth, it is undoubtedly one of the most striking man-made features on the Downs.

One ancient monument has to be mentioned, and that is the South Downs Way itself. We can walk it confident that we are truly on one of the oldest paths in Britain. Something from prehistory that still has a function.

11

The South Downs
East of the Arun

The final section of the walk, covering all of the South Downs between the River Arun and Beachy Head. It is divided into five days' walking.

Walk 16 Arundel to Steyning.
Walk 17 Steyning to Pyecombe.
Walk 18 Pyecombe to Lewes.
Walk 19 Lewes to Alfriston.
Walk 20 Alfriston to Beachy Head.

There are eight circular walks:

Walk 19 Based on Arundel. An eastwards round-trip extending to Chantry Hill above Storrington.

Walk 20 Based on Steyning. A westwards circular walk taking in Chanctonbury Ring.

Walk 21 Based on the Devil's Dyke. A round-trip travelling westwards as far as Tottington Barn above Upper Beeing.

Walk 22 Based on Ditchling Beacon. A westwards round-trip going as far as Wolstonbury Hill.

Walk 23 Using Lewes as a base, a westwards round-trip travelling as far as Blackcap Hill.

Walk 24 Based on Lewes. A circular walk going southwards as far as Rodmell.

Walk 25 Using Alfriston as a base. A round-trip going westwards as far as Firle Beacon.

Walk 26 Based on Alfriston. An eastwards circular walk as far as Beachy Head.

OS maps needed are: 197 Chichester and The Downs;

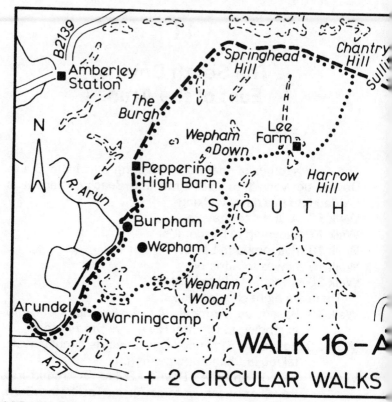

Amberley Station

B2139

The Burgh

N

R. Arun

Springhead Hill

Chantry Hill

Suli

Wepham Down

Lee Farm

Peppering High Barn

Harrow Hill

S O U T H

Burpham

Wepham

Wepham Wood

Arundel

Warningcamp

A27

WALK 16 - A

+ 2 CIRCULAR WALKS

198 Brighton and The Downs; 199 Eastbourne and Hastings.

A long section taking in the very best of walking in Sussex. Rolling hills to travel along and almost continuous far-reaching views across the Weald and out over the coastal plain. There is no walking in the South East to compare with this.

The walks are along the ridgeway path, across the dip slope, below the scarp and in river valleys. The Downs fall into a number of 'blocks' divided up by both dry gaps and river valleys, and these blocks roughly conform to the divisions of the walks so that on each day one tends to

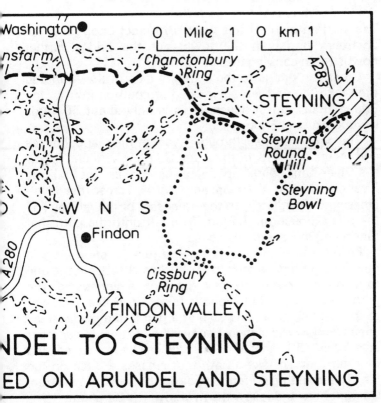

cover the ground between two gaps or to undertake a circular walk within the bounds of one 'block'.

There are both popular and neglected paths used on the walks, and a range of places of specific interest including Cissbury, the Devil's Dyke, the Seven Sisters cliffs and the Long Man of Wilmington.

16th Walk: Arundel to Steyning
Total distance: 14 miles
OS map: 197 Chichester and the Downs; 198 Brighton and the Downs.

Stage 1: Arundel to Chantry Hill

The starting-point of this walk is Arundel Bridge (i.e. the upstream bridge in the town, not the bridge further downstream carrying the A27 bypass).

Cross the bridge to the southern side of the Arun and then take the first left signposted footpath in front of the Bridge House guest-house. (This is only about 50 yards beyond Arundel Bridge.)

The path then goes through a yard at the rear of houses and meets the bank of the Arun. Go right here and follow the river-bank path upstream as far as the railway level-crossing at Warningcamp. Walk across the level-crossing. Immediately on the other side of the railway line there is a house on the left. Turn left onto the path that runs along in front of this house.

Follow the path until you come to a junction. At this point one path goes off into the bushes ahead, but the one to take bears right through a gate and is signposted. The path across the field beyond is faint but visible. Follow it to the next signpost and stile at a gap in the poplar trees ahead. Follow the signpost across the next field to another stile. Walk 150 yards after this stile has been crossed, and then turn left to take a path that crosses a ditch on the left. This route again returns you to the bank of the Arun. Go right here and follow the river towards Burpham.

Follow the Arun as far as a point where a footpath comes in from the right. Go right here, up steps cut in the bank, and follow this path all the way to the road in Burpham by the George and Dragon pub. Turn left at the road and then go right at the first road junction. Follow this road as far as a group of pine trees by Burpham churchyard. Take a path on the right here through the churchyard, leaving the yard by a signposted path in the wall at the far side. (Note: If you take the other path close to this point in error, it leads back into the village.)

The path is a little overgrown, but passable, and should be followed to a road. Turn left at the road. When the road turns left towards Peppering Farm, go straight ahead up the No Through Road, continuing the climb up the Downs dip slope towards the crest.

The road becomes a track at Peppering High Barn. Just past the building here, take a footpath on the right, leaving the bridleway at this point. This is a clear track, concreted for the first short section. The wood on Springhead Hill, the point at which the path reaches the Downs crest, is in clear view ahead. Take the path all the way up to Springhead Hill and go straight ahead at the path junctions encountered on the way up. Just before reaching the wood, once on the top of the hill, the South Downs Way is met. Turn right here and go through the wood.

The path now drops down from Springhead Hill and then climbs again. In the dip between the hills there is a rough car-parking area. From here keep to the right-hand track that runs south of Kithurst Hill, unless you particularly wish to take the longer diversion around beside the triangulation pillar.

Follow the South Downs Way as far as the rough parking-area near Chantry Hill where a road comes up to the Downs crest.

Stage 2: Chantry Hill to Chanctonbury Ring
Continue straight ahead; the path is clear and easy to follow across Sullington Hill. Between Sullington Hill and Barnsfarm Hill there is a slightly confusing path junction. A large barn stands on its own at this point, and the clear, broad path ends. Go past the barn and through a gate, following the signpost up beside a wire fence onto Barnsfarm Hill. The path is scarcely visible. However, once across this large field, the South Downs Way is again a clear track. Now follow this all the way down to the A24 south of Washington.

Cross the A24 (Here you can divert into Washington for a pub lunch if desired, but it is a fairly long diversion.) Turn left on the far side of the A24 and follow the South Downs Way signposting up the steep, rough track towards Chanctonbury Ring. Near the top of the hill there is a junction of tracks. Turn left here and walk to Chanctonbury Ring.

Stage 3: Chanctonbury Ring to Steyning
Follow the clear hilltop path down from Chanctonbury Ring. Go straight ahead at the first path crossroads. (This is where the round-trip walk based on Steyning meets the South Downs Way.) Now follow the Way for about $1\frac{1}{2}$ miles beyond the triangulation pillar above Steyning Round Hill. Go straight on at the path coming in from the right once past the triangulation pillar. At the next junction turn left, leaving the South Downs Way. Care is needed to take the correct path here. The left-hand path goes slightly back on the way you have just come, and is not particularly clear. Do not take the clearer, stony track that runs across this junction. Having found the narrow path, follow it to the next junction. Turn right here, and the route now drops down the side of Steyning Round Hill. Turn left at the path junction part-way down the hill.

At the foot of the hill go right at a path and then follow it a short way to a road. Turn left at the road and follow it all the way into Steyning.

Steyning
Accommodation: This is fairly extensive in the Steyning/- Bramber area.
Public transport: Bus services into Steyning.
Parking: Adequate.

Circular walk based on Arundel (eastwards)
Total distance: 13 miles
OS map: 197 Chichester and The Downs.

Stage 1: Arundel to Chantry Hill
See Stage 1 of the Arundel to Steyning walk.

Stage 2: Chantry Hill to Arundel
Turn right down a bridlepath at the rough car-parking area, leaving the South Downs Way. The path is easy to follow. It runs across the hilltop and then dips into a hollow. In the bottom of the hollow, continue straight on through Lee Farm, ignoring any turn-offs, and follow the track all the way up onto Wepham Down.

Go past a path on the left on Wepham Down and onto the path junction beyond. Here a bridleway forms a crossroads with the path, (it is not an 'offset' junction as the map shows it). Turn left here. The path follows a wire fence around the edge of a field as it descends into the dry valley. At the bottom of the field, go through a gate and continue to follow the fence along the bottom of this quiet, isolated valley. The path is not particularly clear, but it is visible.

At a point roughly below some farm buildings on the right-hand hilltop, the path divides. Either can be taken as they rejoin further along. The path soon begins to become well defined. Go straight on at the crossroads of paths below the farm buildings. A little further on, the path divides, and you should go right here until meeting another path, where you again turn right. The route is now leaving the scrubby area of New Down behind and entering woodland.

Approximately 100 yards on is another junction, where you should go left and walk for 200 yards to another junction. Take the right-hand fork here. This path is waymarked and goes through a field but appears just as a grassy track. After crossing this first field, there is a signposted path junction. Turn left along the wire fence and walk for 50 yards to the next signpost and then continue to follow the fence around. (Do not go left up the hillside.) There is a discernible path along the fence, and the route then enters woodland. Follow the path all the way to a road.

Turn left at the road and walk along it to a crossroads, where you should turn right down a No Through Road. Follow the road all the way to where it ends at the level-crossing met earlier in the day. Turn left on the other side of the railway line and walk along the bank of the Arun back into Arundel.

Circular walk based on Steyning
Total distance: 10 miles
OS map: 198 Brighton and The Downs.

Stage 1: Steyning to Chanctonbury Ring
To leave Steyning find the White Horse pub, at the southern end of the main street along the A283. Beside the White Horse; a road goes off the A283. Take this road. Walk along it beyond the limit of the houses in Steyning and on as the road climbs steeply up onto Steyning Round Hill. Turn right at the road junction near the top of the hill and walk along it. The road levels out as it goes along the side of Steyning Bowl. Walk past the first bridlepath on the right and go on along the road to the next. At this junction there is an iron gate and a signpost indicating the South Downs Way and a public bridleway. Take the bridleway off ahead as it runs diagonally, though indistinctly, across a field. Head for a gateway on the other side of the field.

Once at the gate, go straight across a concrete farm road onto the bridlepath opposite. Cissbury, the objective on this part of the walk, is now in view to the south-west. The path runs very clearly ahead and is to be followed all the way to a crossroads of paths, where you should turn right. Follow this track all the way to a large barn on the left, just below Cissbury. Just past the barn take a path on the left. Follow this to a junction on the right with another

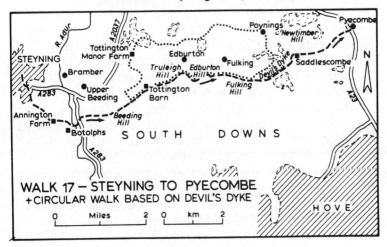

WALK 17 — STEYNING TO PYECOMBE
+ CIRCULAR WALK BASED ON DEVIL'S DYKE

path. Turn right here and walk up to the top of Cissbury.

To leave Cissbury, take the path that goes off to the north, down to the foot of the hill where there is a small car-park. Go straight ahead on a broad track from the car-park. The route is now simple, a gradual climb up the dip slope to the crest of the Downs, going straight ahead at all junctions. Nearing the crest, Chanctonbury Ring comes into view over the left and makes wayfinding easy. On meeting the South Downs Way, turn left and follow it up to Chanctonbury Ring.

Stage 2: Chanctonbury Ring to Steyning
See Stage 3 of the Arundel to Steyning walk.

17th Walk: Steyning to Pyecombe
Total distance: $9\frac{1}{2}$ miles
OS map: 198 Brighton and The Downs

Stage 1: Steyning to Tottington Barn
In order to leave Steyning, it is best to return to the 'White

Horse', the starting-point of the round-trip based on Steyning and the place where the Arundel to Steyning walk meets the A283 at the conclusion of that leg.

From the 'White Horse' walk along the pavement beside the A283 in the direction of Bramber. Walk beyond the older part of the town as far as a road on the right called Maudlin Lane, which is at the Steyning town boundary sign. Go down Maudlin Lane as far as its junction with Annington Road, where you should turn right down Annington Road. Walk along this road beyond Annington Farm and almost as far as Botolphs, take a track on the left signposted as the South Downs Way. The path follows the Adur for a short distance and then crosses it by way of a bridge to meet the A283 beyond.

At the A283 turn left and follow the road for a short distance, then take the first track on the right which goes clearly up to Beeding Hill. On top of Beeding Hill you meet a road. Turn left here and follow the road up to Tottington Barn.

Stage 2: Tottington Barn to Devil's Dyke

The route on this stage of the walk is very simple. Follow the South Downs Way along the crest of the Downs over Edburton Hill, Perching Hill and Fulking Hill with the building on the hilltop above Devil's Dyke in sight ahead most of the way. The pub at the Dyke makes a good lunch-point, so at Fulking Hill divert over to it on one of the paths leading towards it from the Way.

Stage 3: Devil's Dyke to Pyecombe

Walk down the road from the Devil's Dyke pub until past the head of the Devil's Dyke valley. Then turn left onto a clear but unsignposted track. (Ignore the first signposted path on the left that you pass just before this.)

When the track forks, you should bear right. Now stay on this track, keeping straight on at the next junction, following the South Downs Way signpost. You should here be walking parallel to a road.

At the next fork keep to the right, staying close to the road — but do not take any path junctions on the right. Stay on this path across the parking-areas until you go downhill and meet the road at Saddlescombe.

Go straight across the road and along the track on the other side. Pass a house on the right, at which point there is a South Downs Way signpost. Then go through a gate just past a house on the left. This is also signposted.

Turn right at the next signposted junction and proceed through the farm buildings. Once past the farm, go through a gate and then straight ahead, following a South Downs Way signpost uphill. Walk all the way to the top of the hill, continuing straight ahead at the signpost there. Once descending the other side of the hill, you come to another signposted junction (near a dew pond). Turn left here and follow the path down into Pyecombe.

Circular walk based on Devil's Dyke
Total distance: 8 miles
OS map: 198 Brighton and The Downs

Devil's Dyke
A base for the car-owner. There is extensive parking at the Dyke. However, those wishing to use public transport can do so by starting the walk at Poynings, which is served by buses.

Stage 1: Devil's Dyke to Tottington Barn
As a starting point, go to the large car-park behind the pub at Devil's Dyke (i.e. the car-park on the southern side of the pub, not the one at the viewpoint in front of it). From here go down the hillside towards the Dyke. Keep going until you intercept a narrow but well-defined path that runs above the Dyke, along its northern side. Turn left here. The path contours around the hillside and is level,

easy walking. It then begins to descend gradually towards Poynings through woodland.

Emerging from the woodland at the foot of the hill, there is a junction of paths, where you should turn right and walk to the road in Poynings. Turn right at the road and walk through the village past the Royal Oak pub. Walk into the dip of the road beyond the Royal Oak as far as a house called Shepards Hey. Opposite this house, on the left of the road is a gate. Go through the gate. The path then follows a long garden boundary and goes through two swing gates before meeting a road. However, between the second gate and the road there is a path on the left – take this.

On meeting a rough track, turn left. After passing a few houses and ruined farm buildings, the track sets out across open fields. Where the track turns right and peters out in a field, keep on ahead along a narrow footpath. From here the path crosses fields. Although the footpath itself is little used and invisible on the ground, there are stiles to mark the way at each field boundary. Follow these as far as the road near Brook House. Turn right here and follow the road for a short distance before turning left down a private road to Brookside Liveries. Beside the gateway at the start of the private road, a footpath goes off to the left. It is signposted and just negotiable but badly overgrown at first. Follow this path across two paddocks. Go straight ahead where a path joins from the left.

Keep on following the path, waymarked at intervals, until you cross a small stream. Here you turn left and follow the hedge a short distance and then strike out in a right-hand diagonal across the field. (Note: This part is badly defined and waymarked, and following the correct line of the path is really pot-luck – especially if there are standing crops.)

This then comes out at a concrete road south of Perching Sands Farm. Go straight across the road and over the field beyond in a diagonal to the far corner, where there is a signpost and a plank footbridge over a ditch. From here follow a diagonal over the next field to the far corner of the wood ahead.

Once there, you will find a signpost and plank footbridge. Go straight ahead, following the signposts across the fields until you meet a track. Go straight across the track, and follow the signposts through two fields to a junction of paths. Cross a small plank bridge at this point and then take the path running westwards, parallel with the Downs scarp. This crosses a track north of Truleigh Manor Farm and then continues straight ahead, following a field boundary towards a wood.

Follow the path into the wood and keep going as far as a waymarked path crossroads, where you go left.

The path leaves the woods and runs as a green lane, then a surfaced track, until it meets the road at the foot of the Downs at Tottington Manor Farm. Turn right, then almost immediately left at the road onto a signposted path. The path climbs up the scarp, being well signposted and easy to follow.

Approximately three-quarters of the way up the hill there is a wooden gate, at a point where the top of the hill is in view. From here on, the path is unclear, but head towards a signpost just visible on the skyline – although you will lose sight of it when covering the intervening ground. Once at the hilltop, turn right and follow the signpost's direction along a fence until you meet another path. Turn left here through a metal gate. This is now a clear track. Follow the track to a road and turn left to walk to Tottington Barn.

Stage 2: Tottington Barn to Devil's Dyke
See Stage 2 of the Steyning to Pyecombe walk.

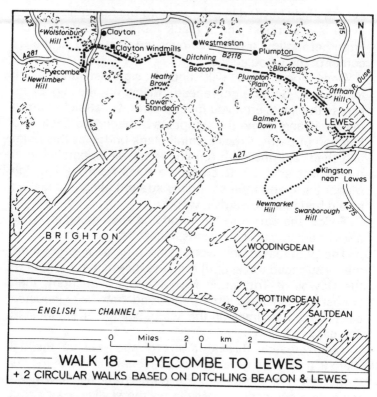

WALK 18 — PYECOMBE TO LEWES
+ 2 CIRCULAR WALKS BASED ON DITCHLING BEACON & LEWES

18th Walk: Pyecombe to Lewes
Total distance: 9 miles
OS map: 198 Brighton and The Downs

Pyecombe
The chief merit of Pyecombe as a base is its accessibility by bus from nearby Brighton and the settlements to the north. For this reason it is best to use parking or accommodation elsewhere and arrive at Pyecombe by bus.

Stage 1: Pyecombe to Clayton Windmills

The starting-point in Pyecombe is near the church. It can be seen on the map that a path runs northwards out of the village. This is the one to take. It starts as a rough track opposite the road junction in Pyecombe beside Dolphin Cottage. It soon narrows to a path.

Continue straight ahead at the first path crossroads and go on to the bridleway a little further along. Turn right here and walk for 200 yards before going first left through a farmyard and across a rough field beyond. Leave the field by its bottom right-hand corner, the path now coming down beside the A23. After a short distance a stile on the right enables you to get down to the road.

Turn right and walk beside the A23 and then leave it by the first turning on the left – a minor road leading up to Clayton Windmills.

Stage 2: Clayton Windmills to Ditchling Beacon

Walk along the track, past the windmills, and where it divides go left on the South Downs Way. From here to Ditchling Beacon it is very straightforward, and a matter of following the main path along the top of the Downs all the way to the road on the top of Ditchling Beacon.

Stage 3: Ditchling Beacon to Blackcap

From the small car-park on the Beacon, go across the road and through the gate opposite. Now simply follow the path along the crest of the Downs. It soon improves to a broad farm track. Walk along it all the way up onto Plumpton Plain and as far as the junction of paths just west of the triangulation pillar on Blackcap.

Stage 4: Blackcap to Lewes

Go straight ahead at this junction, through a gate, leaving the South Downs Way at this point. After 100 yards the track forks. Take the left-hand fork up onto Blackcap, which is a good viewpoint.

Come down from the triangulation pillar and rejoin the path that runs just to the south of the Downs crest. It gradually becomes clearer. Stay on this track until you reach some derelict buildings, some of them used as stables. Here follow the fence ahead until past the enclosed area, taking care not to divert onto the track bearing left over towards Offham Hill.

Once past the buildings, take a path over to the left away from the fence. (Note: You may need to use a compass here to take the correct line, for the path is by no means as clear as the map might suggest, at least in this first section.)

In this first section follow beside a steeplechase course, and in time the path becomes clearer as it descends the hill towards Lewes. Close to the edge of Lewes you join a broad track and follow this ahead into the town.

Lewes
Accommodation: Plentiful.
Public transport: A highly accessible place served by both bus and train.
Parking: Plentiful.

Circular walk based on Ditchling Beacon (westwards)
Total distance: 9 miles
OS map: 198 Brighton and The Downs

Ditchling Beacon
Car-parking is available on Ditchling Beacon (or at Clayton Windmills). For those without a car, this is a difficult walk to undertake. The best idea might be to take a bus out to Ditchling and walk to the Beacon from there, or intercept the walk half-way at Pyecombe.

Stage 1: Ditchling Beacon to Clayton Windmills (via Wolstonbury Hill)

The starting-point of this walk is the car-park on Ditchling Beacon. From here go west along the South Downs Way until about 200 yards beyond the triangulation pillar. Here there is a metal gate in the fence on the left. Go through this and along the path beyond, going through a second gate *en route*. When you come to a third gate, you will be looking down into a dry valley bottom below on the right. The path from here is invisible, but go down into the bottom of the valley and walk through the field as far as a gate in a fence. Go through the gate and continue straight ahead. The path now becomes more distinct, though it is more an animal track than anything else. There is no waymarking.

When you reach the main floor of the Standean Valley, turn left through a gate onto a farm track. As you walk along the track, it gradually becomes more distinct and stony. Follow the track until you come to a path junction at Lower Standean by a large ash tree. Turn right onto the track met here, and after about 200 yards there is at last the reassurance of some waymarking.

Just after passing a lone farm building on the left, the track runs uphill and branches about 50 yards after passing the building. Take the right-hand fork here through a gap in a hedgerow, and follow the path beyond.

Go straight on at the first path junction, a crossroads. From here on the path makes several right-angle turns. At the next junction, turn right and head towards Clayton Windmills beside a golf course until you meet the South Downs Way. Turn left here along the northern side of the golf course all the way down to the A23.

Go straight across the A23 onto the path opposite and follow it close to the A23 until you meet a road on the edge of Pyecombe, where you should go right. Just before reaching the junction in Pyecombe near the church, turn right on a rough track beside Dolphin Cottage, leaving the South Downs Way here. The track soon narrows to a path and should be followed to a junction with a broad track, where you turn left. Follow this route up Wolstonbury Hill all the way to the next path junction. Here go right and follow the footpath up to Wolstonbury Hill fort.

To leave the fort, take the clear path that descends the eastern side of the hill from the triangulation pillar. At the foot of the hill the path meets a track where you should turn right. This leads to a stile in a wire fence. Cross the stile and turn right on the path beyond. After 100 yards you meet the track used to ascend Wolstonbury Hill. Turn left here. Walk for 200 yards and then go first left through a farmyard and across a rough field beyond. Leave the field by its far corner, and the path comes down beside the A23. After a distance a stile on the right enables you to walk down to the A23. Turn right and walk beside the A23 for a short distance, before turning first left on a minor road up to Clayton Windmills.

Stage 2: Clayton Windmills to Ditchling Beacon
See Stage 2 of the Pyecombe to Lewes walk.

Circular walk based on Lewes (westwards)
Total distance: 10 miles
OS map: 198 Brighton and The Downs

Stage 1: Lewes (Southover) to Kingston
See Stage 1 of the Lewes to Alfriston walk.

Stage 2: Kingston to Blackcap
At the top of the hill the track peters out. Keep on straight ahead here until you come to a stile beside a gate. Cross the stile and keep on ahead. From here on, the path is unclear. It runs across the field, roughly following the left-hand fence ahead. In case of any uncertainty here, it

might be as well to follow a compass bearing towards Newmarket Hill until the hill itself comes into view (though the walk will not actually go as far as Newmarket Hill).

Eventually, by following the fence, you will come down to a gate. Go through the gate and continue ahead on a clear track for less than 50 yards before turning right on a path, marked as the South Downs Way, keeping a wire fence to the right. Go down the hill as far as a small wood and then follow the clear path down to the right all the way to the A27 beside the Newmarket pub.

Cross the A27 and take the path on the other side (it starts at the right-hand end of the road-cutting, running up the hillside behind a stand of trees). Follow this path to the top of the field and then through a wood.

On the far side of the wood enter a field through a gate and cross the field to another gate ahead. Once through this gate, turn left and walk beside the wire fence until over the brow of the hill. At the top of the field there is another gate. Go through and maintain the same direction, this time with a fence to the left. The paths here are unclear, but nearing Buckland Bank you are on a clear track.

When you reach the signposted path junction at Buckland Bank, turn right and walk towards the Downs crest up the gentle dip slope. The next path junction encountered is near Blackcap. Turn right here, through a gate, to walk up to Blackcap.

Stage 3: Blackcap to Lewes
See Stage 4 of the Pyecombe to Lewes walk.

Circular walk based on Lewes (southwards)
Total distance: 9 miles
OS map: 198 Brighton and The Downs

The Ouse Gap

The River Ouse is one of a number of major river gaps through the South Downs. It is representative of a particular type of environment, and whilst to some people it is not beautiful, it is full of interest. As so often, the interest begins on the map itself.

On the map it is clear how the presence of an extensive wetland area in the valley bottom has influenced man's use of the land. Note how the roads follow the dry, slightly elevated ground at the foot of the Downs. Both the A275 and B2109 (now the A26) follow such a course on opposite sides of the Gap. Equally, the villages of Iford, Rodmell and Southease have developed on this drier land above the marshes.

It can be seen that the river is tidal in the area of the walk, and at one time most of the low land in the Gap would have been periodically flooded. Human action has modified this. The river channel has been embanked and straightened for navigation and to allow a more rapid run-off of water, and there is a network of drainage ditches all over the Brooks. A clear section of channel cut off by channel straightening can be seen at GR 443032. Normally now the Ouse will not flood because it is controlled.

At one time the Brooks would have been an extensive stretch of reed beds with the Ouse meandering through them. (Much the same picture would have been presented by the other Sussex river gaps.) This began to change a long time ago. By Domesday, Lewes was accessible to sea-going ships, which gives some impression of how the river had been modified even then. Rodmell and Piddinghoe were once fishing villages. As the marsh was gradually drained, these village became farming settlements. Today the Brooks (a local name for marshes) are everywhere farmland. The Middle Ages were the great time of marshland reclamation, and no other Sussex landscape saw as much alteration at this time. However, much of this early work was destroyed by flooding in the late fourteenth and early fifteenth centuries. Reclamation went ahead again later on, and various improvements and maintenance have gone on to this day.

The piecemeal way in which the Brooks have been created comes across on the map in the intricate, irregular pattern of the drainage ditches. This is in contrast to the straight lines of more recent land reclamation elsewhere, where drainage has been undertaken on a big scale.

In draining the marshes to create farmland on the fertile soils, new wildlife habitats have been created. As elsewhere, man has replaced a natural landscape with one that itself supports valuable, but very different, wildlife habitats. Being cut off from the tidal river, the ditches can support a range of freshwater plants and animals. They are of great value because there are very few freshwater habitats left on farms these days. Many ponds and lakes have been drained, filled or polluted, and ditches can often be a last refuge for freshwater wildlife.

The land made available to agriculture by draining the Ouse marshes is almost entirely pasture. Pasture of this type is increasingly rare. Agricultural improvements using underground field drains, chemical weed-control and single-species grass leys are destroying this type of meadow. If it is really well drained, it can even be given over to arable uses. These 'old-style' meadows need to be seen in early summer to appreciate the full range of life the ditches and fields support.

It only needs the land to be drained that bit more efficiently to lose much of its habitat value. It is a delicate balance. Equally, if the land is sometimes submerged by tidewater, as occurs in parts of the lower Cuckmere valley, it becomes a different sort of grassland again.

Stage 1: Lewes (Southover) to River Ouse
See Stages 1 and 2 of the Lewes to Alfriston walk.

Stage 2: River Ouse to Lewes

Navigation is very simple. On meeting the bank of the Ouse, turn left and walk along the embankment path northwards towards Lewes.

It has to be admitted that the final length of the return to Lewes is not the most picturesque (from the A27 road bridge onwards), but it is necessary in order to return from an otherwise scenic round trip.

Go under the A27 road bridge and follow the track away from the river around to the front of the sewage works. (Not making it sound too appealing, am I?) This brings you to a minor road where you should go right. The road runs past school buildings and fields and then comes to a junction. Turn left and you will come to the main road between Southover and Lewes.

19th Walk: Lewes to Alfriston ·

Total distance: 15 miles
OS maps: 198 Brighton and The Downs; 199 Eastbourne and Hastings

Stage 1: Lewes (Southover) to Kingston

The walk begins at Southover on the southern edge of Lewes. Walk to the western end of Southover High Street, where it meets the A275 (GR 408096) by 'The Swan' pub. Walk beyond the pub beside the A275 as far as a turning on the right called Juggs Road. Take this road. Follow the road across a bridge over the A27 and up the hill beyond. When the road becomes a path, simply keep on ahead all the way to Kingston near Lewes.

On meeting the road in Kingston, go straight across and walk along the road opposite. The road becomes a track and climbs steeply up onto the Downs scarp.

Stage 2: Kingston to River Ouse

At the hilltop turn left just before reaching a stile (situated

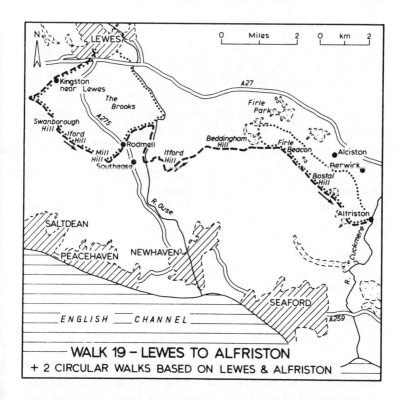

WALK 19 – LEWES TO ALFRISTON
+ 2 CIRCULAR WALKS BASED ON LEWES & ALFRISTON

close to two dewponds) and head towards an area of scrub on the left-hand hilltop. (This in fact marks the position of another dewpond, as you will see on drawing close to it.)

There is a faint path across the grass, and it becomes much clearer once beyond the dewpond. Follow this path all the way to a gate. Go through this and then take a clear track on to Swanborough Hill.

At a point between Swanborough and Iford Hills, where the track turns down to Swanborough Manor, keep straight on with the wire fence to your right along the hilltop. At the far side of this field is a gate with a South Downs Way signpost – follow its direction. You then arrive at a concrete farm road, where you should turn left.

At the far side of Front Hill, the concrete road meets another road which you should cross; go through the gate on the other side. Now go along the grass track towards the clearly visible Mill Hill, crossing another concrete road *en route*. On Mill Hill the path runs beside an extensive hawthorn thicket between two houses and then meets a minor road. Turn left and follow the road down the hill to the A275 at Rodmell. Go left here and then first right beside 'The Holly' pub.

Follow this road down through Rodmell, and where it turns left, continue straight ahead on a track. The track soon comes out onto the Ouse pastures. A ditch runs beside the track, and as the track deteriorates to an ill-defined path nearer the river, use the ditch as a guide towards the Ouse. The last field before reaching the river is entered by a gate; go through this and proceed on to the Ouse embankment.

Stage 3: River Ouse to Firle Beacon

When you meet the Ouse, turn right and follow the river as far as the bridge east of Southease. Cross the bridge and follow the minor road that it carries to Itford Farm beside the main road. (Note: On current OS maps the road is marked as the B2109. In fact it is now upgraded and called the A26)

Turn right at the road and then go first left onto the clear track up Itford Hill. Roughly halfway up the hill there is a concrete waymarking plinth. Turn left here, leaving the track, following now a path of grass.

Breasting the top of Itford Hill, you catch sight of the masts on Beddingham Hill ahead. It is for these that you now aim. A wire fence runs to the right of the path all the way from Itford Hill to Beddingham Hill as a help to staying on the correct path.

When you reach the masts on Beddingham Hill, simply maintain the same direction on the track, setting the course now on the distant rise of Firle Beacon. On the far side of the field in which the masts are situated, there is a gate. Go through this and continue straight ahead. Again, a wire fence runs to the right of the path.

Just after passing a covered reservoir on the left, you meet a road. Go straight across the road and into the rough parking-area on the other side. Go through the small gate on the far side of the car-park. From here follow the path of worn sward up onto Firle Beacon.

Stage 4: Firle Beacon to Alfriston
From Firle Beacon continue in the same direction, following the line of the fence on the right-hand side. Continue straight ahead through the farm buildings in the hollow between Firle Beacon and Bostal Hill, and then keep on ahead on a clear track up to Bostal Hill.

On the eastern side of Bostal Hill the path is less clear, but visible. When you come to a gate through the fence, go through and continue ahead on the other side on a clear track.

At Long Burgh there is a confusing and badly waymarked path junction. Go straight ahead on a short stretch of narrow path until you come to a broad track. This track then runs clearly down into Alfriston.

Circular walk based on Alfriston (westwards)
Total distance: 8 miles
OS maps: 199 Eastbourne and Hastings; 198 Brighton and The Downs

Stage 1: Alfriston to Firle Beacon
The walk begins at the stone cross in the village centre. From here leave the village by the road going off the square between the Market Inn and a newsagents (signposted to the car-park). Once level with the car-park, the road forks and you should take the left fork at this

point. Now follow this road beyond the edge of Alfriston until you arrive at a crossroads formed by two tracks meeting the road at a sharp right-hand bend. Go straight ahead down a track at this point.

From here stay on this track. There are several junctions coming in to meet it, but keep straight on at all of them, walking roughly parallel with the scarp of the Downs all the time. The point to begin paying more attention to route-finding is once you come into sight of a single hilltop tower ahead and to the right of the path. This should come into view shortly after the path crossroads south of Tilton Farm.

You are now drawing closer to the foot of the scarp, and when you draw roughly level with the tower, the path branches in front of a cottage. Take the left fork at this point. Go past the junction on the right further on. A little further on you come to a rather confusing meeting of tracks and paths. Turn left here, towards the Downs, up a path following the field edge beside woodland. About halfway up the hill there is a gate across the path. Go through and follow the path up to the scarp top and so up onto Firle Beacon.

Stage 2: Firle Beacon to Alfriston
See Stage 4 of the Lewes to Alfriston walk.

20th Walk: Alfriston to Beachy Head
Total distance: 9 miles
OS map: 199 Eastbourne and Hastings

Alfriston
Accommodation: Plentiful.
Public transport: Served by bus.
Parking: Free car-park in the village.

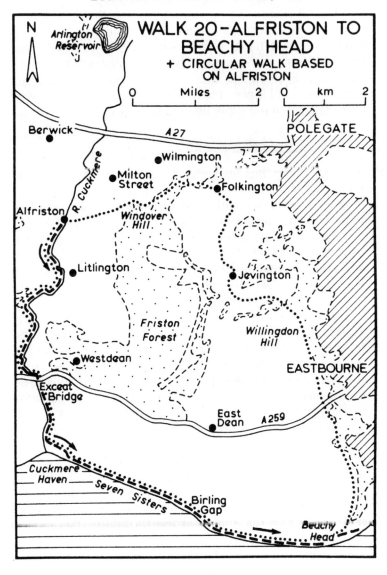

WALK 20–ALFRISTON TO BEACHY HEAD
+ CIRCULAR WALK BASED ON ALFRISTON

To leave Alfriston, go to the bank of the River Cuckmere where it runs past the village. From here you follow the river, on either bank, southwards all the way to Exceat Bridge. However, the western bank is probably the best one to use because on this side of the river you can reach the viewpoint of High and Over. (This is some way downstream of Alfriston, beyond Litlington.)

Diversion onto High and Over
The viewpoint is worth visiting, and because the map is unclear, I have included this detail on how to climb the hill.

Walk along the western embankment of the Cuckmere until almost beyond the southern end of the hill (i.e. beyond the chalk horse cut in its side). Now look for a stile on the path ahead. Do not cross the stile, but turn right and cross a small ditch by the plank footbridge provided. Now take the defined path up the side of the hill to the top. Return to the river by the same route.

Beyond High and Over, the path on the west of the Cuckmere becomes less clear, but it is visible and can be followed to the A259. On meeting this road, turn left and follow it down to Exceat Bridge. At Exceat Bridge cross the road and go down to the river again. But this time follow the eastern bank of the Cuckmere towards Cuckmere Haven (if you follow the western bank down, expecting to find a bridge at the mouth of the river, you are in for a shock!)

Once you reach the beach at Cuckmere Haven, turn left and follow the path behind the beach towards the first of the Seven Sisters cliffs at Cliff End. A stile enables you to reach the hillside and climb up onto the cliff top. As with the route down the course of the Cuckmere, this half of the walk is very simple to navigate. Simply follow the roller-coaster backs of the chalk along the cliff-top path, keeping the sea to the right all the way to Beachy Head.

Beachy Head is the end of the whole long-distance

walk. Time, then, to ask if it has all been worthwhile. If you have come all the way from Dover and are on Beachy Head reading this, then the answer has to be yes. Otherwise you would have dumped your rucksack off the Medway Bridge weeks ago.

Circular walk based on Alfriston (eastwards)
Total distance: 18 miles
OS Map: 199 Eastbourne and Hastings

Stage 1: Alfriston to Beachy Head
See the Alfriston to Beachy Head walk.

Stage 2: Beachy Head to Alfriston
There are many ways of returning to Alfriston from Beachy Head, but, because this is intended to be a small book, I will describe only one. It is the longest of the options available but probably the most interesting.

From the various buildings at Beachy Head, a minor road with very broad verges runs northwards. Follow this road along the right-hand verge as far as the point where it meets the B2103. Opposite the junction of these two roads there is a clearly defined path cut through the high scrub. Take this path and follow it until you meet some concrete waymarkers close to a stony track. Join this track and follow it northwards, passing after a while a triangulation pillar and concrete-lined dewpond on the right.

On meeting the A259, go straight across onto the clear track opposite. Stay on this track, ignoring any others that run beside it in places. Go straight ahead at any path junctions, staying on the track all the way to Jevington.

When you meet the road through Jevington, turn right and walk to the northern edge of the village until you arrive at a track on the left opposite a house called the 'Old Post Office'. Follow this track for some way until a path joins it from the right. (Note: On the map this path appears to be a broader, clearer one than in fact it is. In reality it is narrow and easily missed.)

Turn right onto this path and walk along it as far as the church at Folkington.

When you reach the church, take the left-hand path which joins opposite the corner of the churchyard wall. The path skirts the edge of a field and then becomes wider. It runs through woodland most of the way, and just before leaving the last stretch of woodland there is an iron gate on the left. Go through the gate, leaving the wider path. The path now is narrow and less well defined, but easy enough to follow as it runs along the contour of the scarp. It arrives below the Long Man of Wilmington after some distance.

Beyond the Long Man, join the worn track which curves away to the west of the chalk figure. This brings you to a gate. At this point a clear track goes down to the right, but do not take this. Instead go through the gate and follow a wire fence until it can be crossed by a stile. Fifty yards beyond the stile you meet a sunken track. Turn right here and follow the track downhill, crossing a road on the way. A hundred yards beyond the road crossing there is a stile on the left of the track. Go over this and take a diagonal path across the fields towards Alfriston, the spire of the church clear ahead. Stay on this path until you meet a road. Cross the road to the footpath opposite and walk along it to the Cuckmere beside Alfriston – the starting-point of the day's walk.

Select Bibliography

Brandon, Peter, *The Sussex Landscape* (Hodder & Stoughton, 1974)

Fullager, A.P. and Virgo, H.E., *Map Reading and Local Studies in Colour* (Hodder & Stoughton, 1975)

Jennet, Sean, *South Downs Way* (HMSO, 1977)

Muir, Richard, *Shell Guide to Reading the Landscape* (Michael Joseph, 1981)

Stamp, L. Dudley, *Britain's Structure and Scenery* (Collins, 1960)

Wright, Christopher, *A Guide to the Pilgrims' Way and North Downs* (Constable and Co Ltd, 1971)

Index